REDEEMING
Your Phone Time

A BIBLE STUDY COMPANION FROM
THE DAILY GRACE CO.

MIRANDA MAE EWING

Table of Contents

Do you remember when smartphones took the world by storm? Long gone were days of flip phones and other older phone models. Smartphones were new, magical, sophisticated pieces of technology that revolutionized the idea of the basic cell phone. With their numerous apps and fun features, the phones drew in consumers by the millions. These pieces of technology have changed our society so tremendously that generations to come will have little idea what life was like without a smartphone.

However, for all the positives things smartphones bring to our lives, there are also negative sides to owning smartphones. For one, we have lost life rhythms. Families must now fight for screen-free evenings and family dinners. Reading books seems a greater challenge with shortened attention spans. Social media serves as the main avenue for people to connect, while real-life, in-person connections are often forgotten. Honest, empathetic conversations between acquaintances, friends, and even family members who disagree are seemingly declining. Even more importantly, there are now many more distractions between us and spending time with the Lord.

Do not be fooled. The battle to spend time in the Word of God did not begin with the rise of technology, but the enemy surely loves taking seemingly innocent things and turning them into slow-growing, hidden poisons that seek to destroy our love of Christ and His Word. And that is why we must learn how to use technology in a way that honors Him. We easily take good things and misuse them for our selfish purposes. And are not our smartphones too often used to satisfy our needs and desires?

This thirty-day challenge allows you to reevaluate how you use your smartphone—not to eradicate it from your life entirely but to guide you in sanctifying how you use it.

The first five days of the challenge present various problems that arise in the misuse of our devices, while the second five days will aid you in making a plan for spending intentional time on your phone. Finally, the last twenty days will provide helpful advice, tips, and encouragement as you begin implementing your plan.

As you work this thirty-day challenge, remember that your efforts to give your screen time to the Lord do not earn His favor or pleasure. If you believe in Jesus, you are covered in the righteousness of Christ. The desire to form holy habits with your device can be carried out because of your love for God and not from fear of disappointing Him.

So as you struggle in this endeavor, rest in Him, and know He loves you and is well-pleased because of the work of Jesus Christ on the cross. Let's get started!

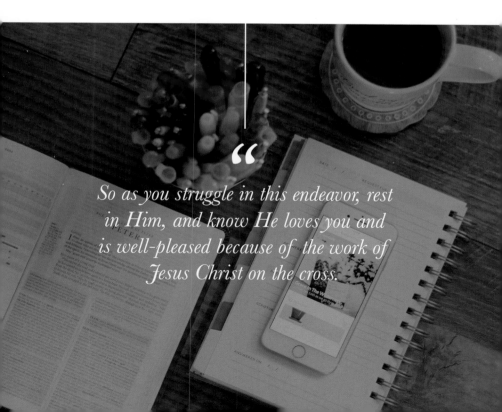

So as you struggle in this endeavor, rest in Him, and know He loves you and is well-pleased because of the work of Jesus Christ on the cross.

Heavenly Father,

As I begin this challenge to redeem my phone time and use it for Your glory, help me to live in light of eternity. Let me view my phone as a tool that can bring me closer to You. Help me also be aware of how it can draw me away from You. Father, let my time spent with You in Your Word be my anchor and true joy, and let my time on my phone be an afterthought in comparison. Thank you for my union with Jesus, my Savior and friend, who gives me strength, wisdom, peace, and rest. Thank You that seeking to live in obedience to You does not achieve my salvation, for my salvation has already been accomplished through Christ. Help me to rely on You and give You glory on both the good and hard days of this challenge. I am so excited to love You more by bringing my phone under Your control. You are a good and gracious Father, and I am thankful to be Yours forever.

Amen.

DAILY GOALS

	1	2	3	4	5	6	7	8	9	10	11

MONTHLY GOALS

12	13	14	15	16	17	18	19	20	21	22	23	24	25	26	27	28	29	30

WEEKLY GOALS

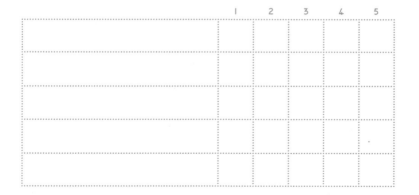

	1	2	3	4	5

week 1

DAY	TOTAL SCREEN TIME	3 MOST USED APPS	TIME SPENT ON EACH
MON			
TUE			
WED			
THU			
FRI			
SAT			

What is one way that time away from my phone has helped me grow in Christ?

_____

_____

_____

What is one way that using my phone has helped me grow in Christ?

_____

_____

_____

HOW I HONORED THE LORD WITH MY PHONE TODAY	HOW I COULD IMPROVE IN MY PHONE TIME	✓

What mistakes did I make this week with my phone, and what changes do I need to make in order to improve next week?

_____

_____

_____

_____

_____

_____

_____

week 2

DAY	TOTAL SCREEN TIME	3 MOST USED APPS	TIME SPENT ON EACH
MON			
TUE			
WED			
THU			
FRI			
SAT			

What is one way that time away from my phone has helped me grow in Christ?

_____

_____

_____

What is one way that using my phone has helped me grow in Christ?

_____

_____

_____

HOW I HONORED THE LORD WITH MY PHONE TODAY	HOW I COULD IMPROVE IN MY PHONE TIME	✔

What mistakes did I make this week with my phone, and what changes do I need to make in order to improve next week?

_____

_____

_____

_____

_____

_____

_____

week 3

DAY	TOTAL SCREEN TIME	3 MOST USED APPS	TIME SPENT ON EACH
MON			
TUE			
WED			
THU			
FRI			
SAT			

What is one way that time away from my phone has helped me grow in Christ?

_____

_____

_____

What is one way that using my phone has helped me grow in Christ?

_____

_____

_____

HOW I HONORED THE LORD WITH MY PHONE TODAY	HOW I COULD IMPROVE IN MY PHONE TIME	✓

What mistakes did I make this week with my phone, and what changes do I need to make in order to improve next week?

_____

_____

_____

_____

_____

_____

_____

week 4

DAY	TOTAL SCREEN TIME	3 MOST USED APPS	TIME SPENT ON EACH
MON			
TUE			
WED			
THU			
FRI			
SAT			

What is one way that time away from my phone has helped me grow in Christ?

_____

_____

_____

What is one way that using my phone has helped me grow in Christ?

_____

_____

_____

HOW I HONORED THE LORD WITH MY PHONE TODAY	HOW I COULD IMPROVE IN MY PHONE TIME	✔

What mistakes did I make this week with my phone, and what changes do I need to make in order to improve next week?

_____

_____

_____

_____

_____

_____

_____

_____

What are Your Whys?

When you begin developing a healthier habit, it is easy to become discouraged in the struggle and revert to your old ways. Sometimes, people are discouraged from changing something about themselves because they fear that they will never get it right or will just fail again. All change involves failure because we are human beings, but because we are human, we are also not incapable of change. The only One who never changes and remains completely the same is the Lord. The Lord constantly transforms us to be more like Christ. So as you may struggle in this challenge of redeeming your phone time, accept your failures and mistakes; take them to the Lord. His strength is sufficient for your weakness, and He is well pleased with a humble heart seeking earnestly to love Him.

To help you in these moments of struggle, write down a few of your "whys." See the provided examples, and then list some of your own. Looking back at these throughout the challenge will help encourage you to persevere and not give up!

EXAMPLES OF "WHYS":

1. To love the Lord more than any device

2. To be healthily present with my friends and family

3. To show my children in a technology-driven world that my time spent in the Word is much more important than time spent on my phone

4. To use all the wonderful resources on my phone well so that it can be a tool to help grow my faith rather than hinder it

This is why:

Encouraging Verses
for redeeming your phone time

COMMIT YOUR ACTIVITIES TO
THE LORD, AND YOUR PLANS
WILL BE ESTABLISHED.

PROVERBS 16:3

DON'T STORE UP FOR YOURSELVES
TREASURES ON EARTH, WHERE MOTH AND
RUST DESTROY AND WHERE THIEVES BREAK
IN AND STEAL. BUT STORE UP FOR YOUR-
SELVES TREASURES IN HEAVEN, WHERE
NEITHER MOTH NOR RUST DESTROYS, AND
WHERE THIEVES DON'T BREAK IN AND
STEAL. FOR WHERE YOUR TREASURE IS,
THERE YOUR HEART WILL BE ALSO.

MATTHEW 6:19-21

LOVE THE LORD YOUR GOD WITH ALL
YOUR HEART, WITH ALL YOUR SOUL,
AND WITH ALL YOUR STRENGTH.

DEUTERONOMY 6:5

GUARD YOUR HEART ABOVE ALL ELSE,
FOR IT IS THE SOURCE OF LIFE.

PROVERBS 4:23

PAY CAREFUL ATTENTION, THEN, TO HOW
YOU LIVE-NOT AS UNWISE PEOPLE BUT
AS WISE-MAKING THE MOST OF THE
TIME, BECAUSE THE DAYS ARE EVIL.

EPHESIANS 5:15-16

AND I WILL ASK THE FATHER, AND HE
WILL GIVE YOU ANOTHER COUNSELOR TO
BE WITH YOU FOREVER. HE IS THE SPIRIT
OF TRUTH. THE WORLD IS UNABLE TO
RECEIVE HIM BECAUSE IT DOESN'T SEE
HIM OR KNOW HIM. BUT YOU DO KNOW
HIM, BECAUSE HE REMAINS WITH YOU
AND WILL BE IN YOU.

JOHN 14:16-17

PART
01

The
PROBLEM

IT IS GOOD,
MEANINGFUL
WORK TO
DEVELOP
SELF-CONTROL.

Have You Noticed?

The rain hits against your bedroom window, gently pulling you from your sleep and causing you to shift and sigh in bed. A new day is beginning. Your mind starts racing as you consider everything you need to do, and it becomes overwhelming. Out of habit, your hand automatically reaches for your nightstand, where your trusty smartphone waits for you. Your eyes are still tired, yet you feel no choice but to greet your dear technological friend. This handy little box that you carry around each day spends more time with you than anyone else. It is always there to make you smile, help pass the free time, rest with you after work, search for random pieces of information, order something online, and even give you directions to get somewhere. It seems you need the device for everything. What would you do without it?

Have you noticed how many times you pick up your phone each day? Have you noticed that you feel slightly panicked or worried without it nearby when you lose your phone? Have you noticed that you might sometimes look at the screen of your phone more than the face of a loved one or friend? Have you noticed that often it is more appealing to look at your phone than sit before the Lord in His Word? Have you noticed?

If this booklet is in your hands, it likely means you have noticed some of these habits mentioned above and want to change how you approach your smartphone. Perhaps you think that it will be rather difficult to stop some of your habits. And you are right—it will be.

But it is good, meaningful work to develop self-control over something that has a dangerous amount of influence in our lives.

And we are not incapable of change. Only the Lord stays the same forever. We change every day as we follow Him and grow in Christ-likeness. It is possible to make different decisions when it comes to your phone, but you should understand what is at stake so that it genuinely matters to you. To accomplish your goal, you must have a plan!

To accomplish your goal, you must have a plan!

WHAT ARE THE GREATEST NEGATIVE IMPACTS YOUR PHONE HAS HAD ON YOUR LIFE?

- Filling up my "down" moments
- Distracting me from everyday life & relationships
- Not letting me be bored

WHEN YOU THINK OF WHERE YOU WILL BE A YEAR FROM NOW, WHAT DO YOU HOPE WILL BE DIFFERENT ABOUT YOUR PHONE HABITS?

- That I won't check it so often or feel that urge

WRITE A SIMPLE PRAYER TO THE LORD, ASKING HIM FOR HIS STRENGTH AND HELP AS YOU BEGIN THIS CHALLENGE.

Abba - would you guide me in my use of my phone. Would you change me anyway I need to be changed?
I invite & welcome you to.

IN THEIR VERY
DESIGN, OUR
PHONES HAVE
BECOME
DISTRACTIONS
TO US.

What is Distraction Doing to You?

Summer break is a favorite time of year for most elementary school children. School is out, the weather is beautiful, and the sun warms the day. You can spend your time relaxing at home, taking walks to the neighborhood pool, or going to the movies. Maybe you remember participating in summer reading programs through your school or library, as this season can provide endless opportunities to get lost in the pages of a book.

Yet, whether you are a reader or not, you can probably admit to the fact that reading comprehension and scenarios similar to the one described above have taken significant tolls in recent years because of smartphones. Rarely do people sit uninterrupted with books for hours on end without feeling the itch to check their phones. In their very design, our phones have become distractions to us.

And while we could discuss the myriad of ways our phones distract us, perhaps the more important thing to highlight is what this distraction can do to our spirits. When the things of this world constantly distract us, we repeatedly set our minds on things that do not last instead of on the things above (Colossians 3:2). Consider Romans 8:5-6: "For those who live according to the flesh have their minds set on the things of the flesh, but those who live according to the Spirit have their minds set on the things of the Spirit. Now the mindset of the flesh is death, but the mindset of the Spirit is life and peace." As human beings who live in this world, it makes sense that we will engage with the things of this earth. However, we must be careful not to allow worldly things to consume us.

When we allow the things of this world to constantly distract us, we deny ourselves a mindset of life and peace, failing to develop spiritual disciplines like solitude, meditation on God's Word, and prayer. All three of these disciplines most certainly give life and peace as they ground us in the reality that God is always with us, and His Word is ours as a guide through life.

Our phones constantly distract us as we subconsciously convince ourselves that we need them more than anything else. For some, they have become an idol that can so easily keep us from knowing God more intimately. Let us remember that it is only in Him that we have everything we need.

Let us remember that it is only in Him that we have everything we need.

Day Two Questions

TRY AND SPEND FIFTEEN MINUTES TODAY IN SILENCE WITHOUT YOUR PHONE AND WITH YOUR BIBLE. READ PSALM 119:9-16.

DOES THE ATTITUDE OF THE PSALMIST REFLECT YOUR DISPOSITION TOWARD GOD'S WORD? WHY OR WHY NOT?

TRY PUTTING YOUR PHONE AWAY FOR AN HOUR, AND COUNT HOW MANY TIMES YOU WANT TO LOOK AT IT. PRAY EACH TIME YOU THINK OF YOUR PHONE THAT YOU WILL DESIRE THE LORD AND HIS WORD MORE.

IF WE DO NOT
CONTROL OUR
PHONE HABITS,
THEY CAN BECOME
ALL-CONSUMING.

The Approval of Man

As human beings created in the image of God, we are made for relationships with others. This need for relationships also creates a desire within us to be seen and known. While this desire is only perfectly satisfied in being known by God, we still seek out man's approval to try and appease it. The problem is that no matter how many people make us feel seen or validated, it will never be enough. There will always be someone else we want to please or whose attention we want to win.

The worlds that our phones have created can tend to pull us deeper into a self-absorbed pit. They invite us to set up our own little kingdoms through social media. In these kingdoms of our making, we decide what people see about us, and we can connect with almost anyone in the world who is on social media. Historically, most people were only connected to 100-150 people at any given time in their lives. However, today, our phones allow us to connect with millions of people—all the more people to please!

Researchers have also found that our bodies release dopamine whenever we experience positive, social stimuli through social media. The more we interact positively on social media, the more we train our brains to need this form of connection and online approval. No wonder anxiety and depression have increased in the last few years! People in our online world consume our thoughts. We struggle with troubling questions and ideas like: *Why did the picture I post not receive as many likes as I thought it would? I wonder why some people stopped following me—did I do something wrong? If only I had as many followers as he does. If only people loved me as they love her.* These thoughts and questions can go on and on. And if we do not control our phone habits, they can become all-consuming.

But the beautiful truth found in the gospel is that when we follow Christ, we are completely accepted and loved by the King of kings. Christ clothes us in His righteousness, and He has made His home in us. Would it not be better to dwell more on this truth? The One who made the universe knows you intimately and will always see you. There is not a place you can go where your presence would be unknown to Him.

So you can turn off your phone and relinquish the desire to be known by the world, for your Creator is well pleased with you, and He wants you to know Him. Man's approval will never be enough, and it pales in comparison to the approval of God.

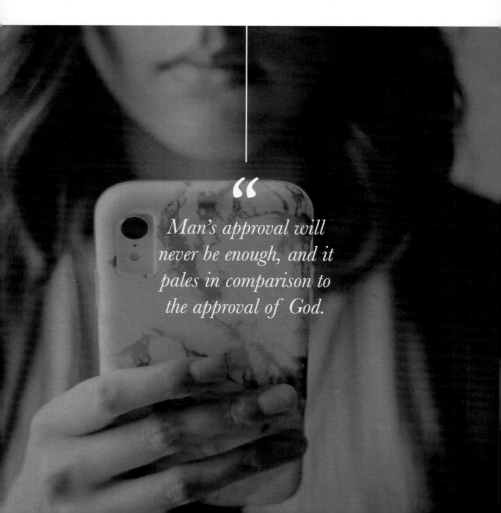

" Man's approval will never be enough, and it pales in comparison to the approval of God.

Day Three Questions

IN WHAT WAYS DO YOU SEEK THE APPROVAL OF MAN THROUGH THE USE OF YOUR PHONE?

Texting w/ Chip - His responses make me feel seen, heard, loved - connected.
Really gaurding what I share & don't share.

IN AN EFFORT TO PLEASE OTHERS, HAVE YOU NOTICED ANY NEGATIVE HABITS IN YOURSELF?

HOW DOES THE KNOWLEDGE THAT THE LORD IS WELL PLEASED WITH YOU INFLUENCE YOUR CARE FOR HOW OTHERS SEE YOU?

Is that enough for me?

YOUR PHONE IS SHAPING YOU, WHETHER YOU LIKE IT OR NOT.

Transforming
Your Mind

In Romans 12:2, Paul directs the church of Romans to "not be conformed to this age, but be transformed by the renewing of your mind, so that you may discern what is the good, pleasing, and perfect will of God." What we set our minds on—those things that hold our attention—are what conform us. Slowly but surely, we become more like the people or ideas we focus on, and often we do not even realize it. The implications of this truth can be frightening if our attention has been misplaced. For example, when we observe our current cultural climate, we see how prone many people are to anxiety or anger regarding a news story or political event. This can happen when we saturate ourself with news from our devices.

It is not wrong to be informed about what is happening in the world around us. In fact, as followers of Jesus, being informed can greatly aid us in our evangelistic conversations and how we pray. However, if we dedicate most of our affection to learning about current events, the voices we listen to will shape us—informing our thoughts, feelings, and passions.

Consider the voices you hear on your device and the time you spend giving them your attention. Your phone is shaping you, whether you like it or not; it is either drawing you closer to Jesus or further away from Him. Be honest with yourself, and ask if the time you spend in God's Word is less than the time you spend scrolling on your phone. For many of us, that answer will be a resounding "yes," and we must acknowledge that this is not healthy or a good use of our time. However, we can use our phones to focus more on the Lord and His Word. Phones can indeed become tools rather than hindrances.

At the end of our lives, we will likely not wish we spent more time on our devices. However, we might wish that we had spent more time with our families, the Lord, and His Word. Learning how to use your phone wisely will directly impact the person you are becoming, and it will also help you not to neglect what matters most.

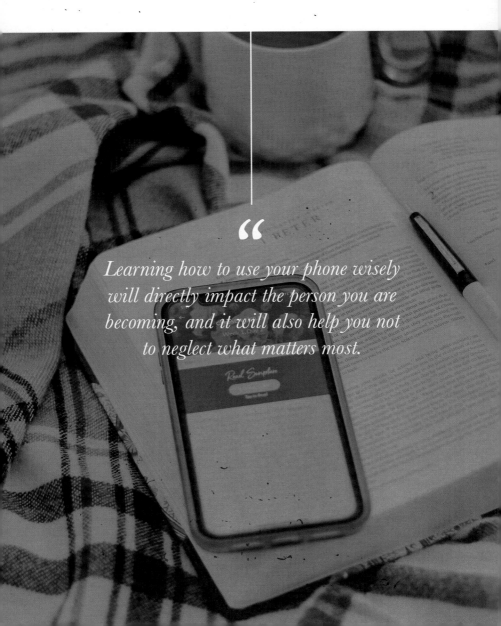

Learning how to use your phone wisely will directly impact the person you are becoming, and it will also help you not to neglect what matters most.

Day Four Questions

WHAT THREE THINGS DO YOU TEND TO FOCUS ON MOST IN YOUR LIFE? (THESE MAY NOT ALL BE THINGS ON YOUR PHONE!)

- Texting - checking
- Learning truth/Seeking God
- Self-care

HOW DO THE THINGS YOU LISTED ABOVE TEND TO MAKE YOU FEEL? HAVE YOU NOTICED ANY NEGATIVE TENDENCIES BECAUSE OF THE FEELINGS YOU HAVE BEEN HAVING?

Texting - I feel bad when I see noone has texted me or not texted me back or I feel bad when I haven't.

WHAT SORT OF POSITIVE CHANGES COULD HAPPEN IN YOUR LIFE FROM FOCUSING ON THE WORD OF GOD MORE THAN YOUR PHONE?

It will liberate me from finding my worth as a person based on if others have thought of me or taken the time to respond to me.

WE IDOLIZE OUR
DEVICES AND LOOK
TO THEM TO FULFILL
A NEED ONLY THE
LORD CAN SATISFY.

Using Your Phone Well

The last few days have required you to reflect on the habits and practices you have with your phone. While it is not easy to admit some of the negative ways our phones have impacted us, it is instrumental in our movement toward change and growth. The reality is that we as humans are prone to idolatry. From the beginning of God's redemptive plan with His chosen people, human beings have tried to make gods out of things that do not deserve their worship. They have also tried to set themselves up as gods. We often do both of these things when we spend too much time with our phones. We idolize our devices and look to them to fulfill a need only the Lord can satisfy. And we sometimes attempt having people worship us through the use of different social media platforms, where we set up our profiles as highlight reels of our lives to show others how great we are.

Perhaps you suspect the message here is that we should just throw our phones away and forget about them, but that is not the message. Phones are not inherently evil. They are not the problem. The problem resides in the heart of the user. Listen to the words of Jesus from Matthew 15:11-20:

> It's not what goes into the mouth that defiles a person, but what comes out of the mouth—this defiles a person... Don't you realize that whatever goes into the mouth passes into the stomach and is eliminated? But what comes out of the mouth comes from the heart, and this defiles a person. For from the heart come evil thoughts, murders, adulteries, sexual immoralities, thefts, false testimonies, slander. These are the things that defile a person; but eating with unwashed hands does not defile a person.

Our hearts are the problem! We have hearts that can easily twist everything around us for evil because we are sick with sin. It is our sinful nature that causes us to use our phones incorrectly. However, because we have the righteousness of Christ and have been made new, we can use them in ways that honor the Lord. In fact, we must understand how to use our devices wisely because they are not going anywhere. As time goes on and technology continues to advance, we see phones becoming more addictive and distracting. So what do we do—how do we change? The answer lies in 2 Corinthians 12:9-10:

> But He said to me, "My grace is sufficient for you, for my power is perfected in weakness." Therefore, I will most gladly boast all the more about my weaknesses, so that Christ's power may reside in me. So I take pleasure in weaknesses, insults, hardships, persecutions, and in difficulties, for the sake of Christ. For when I am weak, then I am strong.

Realize your weakness, and bask in the power and glory of Christ. He will show you the way. He will take your inability and show you how He is perfectly able to make you more like Him. The problem that so many of us have with our devices invite us to learn how to use them rightly and glorify the Lord through their use. Let us trust Him to help us as we seek to change, allowing our phones to become tools that help us love the Lord and others more.

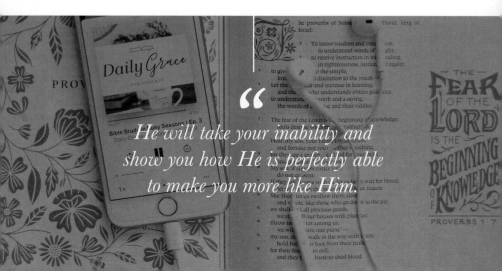

He will take your inability and show you how He is perfectly able to make you more like Him.

DO YOU RECOGNIZE ANY FORM OF IDOLATRY IN THE WAY THAT YOU USE YOUR PHONE? HOW HAS IT CAUSED YOU TO WORSHIP SOMETHING OR SOMEONE OTHER THAN THE LORD?

JESUS'S WORDS IN MATTHEW 15 TEACH US THAT OUR HEARTS DEFILE US. BESIDES YOUR PHONE, WHAT THINGS CAN YOU BE TEMPTED TO BLAME FOR YOUR SIN INSTEAD OF YOUR OWN HEART?

WRITE A PRAYER TO THE LORD, ASKING FOR HIS POWER TO BE MADE PERFECT IN YOUR WEAKNESS. ASK HIM TO HELP YOU USE MOMENTS OF WEAKNESS WITH YOUR PHONE FOR HIS GLORY!

Making
A PLAN

OUR MOTIVATION
FOR HAVING
SELF-CONTROL
WITH OUR DEVICES
IS SO THAT WE CAN
LOVE GOD MORE.

Taking Time
to Evaluate

As we begin the second part of our challenge, let us slow down and
evaluate our phone habits. This part of the challenge will require
you to be honest with yourself and admit to some things that may
feel embarrassing or shameful. But remember, our motivation for
having self-control with our devices is so that we can love God
more. We are not trying to earn His love. As His adopted sons and
daughters covered in His righteousness, we already have it. Today
you will work through a series of questions that will help you make
a plan to use your phone differently. These questions will require
you to reflect for at least fifteen to twenty minutes. If right now
is not the time you can do that properly, choose a different time
today, and come back to the questions.

Before you begin, put your phone away in another room, and
just sit in silence. Close your eyes, and tell the Lord, "Father, I
need You. Help me honor you and love you more." Open your
Bible to Psalm 16. Read through the Psalm, and pray it to the
Lord. If you are unsure how to do that, here is an example you
can follow for verses 1-2:

*"Protect me, God, for I take refuge in you. I said to the Lord, 'You
are my Lord; I have nothing good besides you.'"*

*Lord, preserve me as I take refuge in You and rely on Your strength
in using my phone and time well. Help me to see that You are mine,
and I am Yours. Without You, there is no good in my life, but with
You, everything becomes sweeter and better. Help me realize that
there is no goodness on my phone that is better than what I can
find in You. Help me to use my phone in a way that allows me to
discover how good You truly are.*

After you have finished praying and sitting in silence, grab your
phone and a pencil to answer the following questions:

Day Six Questions

LOOK AT THE SCREEN TIME ON YOUR PHONE. YOU WILL FIND THIS UNDER YOUR SETTINGS. WRITE DOWN THE FOLLOWING:

DAILY AVERAGE OF SCREEN TIME: 5 hours!

TOTAL WEEKLY AMOUNT OF SCREEN TIME: 25 hours

TOTAL AMOUNT OF TIME USED ON SOCIAL APPS: 11 hours

TOP THREE APPS USED: messages
Safari
podcasts

HOW MANY TIMES YOU PICK UP YOUR PHONE: 33 a day
166 per week

REFLECT ON THE NUMBERS YOU HAVE WRITTEN. WHICH STATISTICS CONCERN YOU THE MOST?

I'm using my phone 5 hours out of the day!
2 hours a day on messages!
Oh my gosh!

WHAT IS THE FIRST APP YOU OPEN WHEN YOU GRAB YOUR PHONE?

messages

HOW DO THE APPS THAT YOU USE THE MOST BRING GLORY TO GOD? HOW DO THEY NOT BRING GLORY TO GOD?

Bring? When I encourage my friends or ~~they~~ encourage me spiritually through text messages.

Not? When I'm texting Chip. Or just checking messages when I don't need to so frequently.

HOW MUCH TIME DO YOU SPEND IN GOD'S WORD AND PRAYER EACH DAY? HOW DOES THIS COMPARE TO THE TIME YOU SPEND ON YOUR PHONE EACH DAY?

90 minutes a day - It's far less

WHEN IS THE FIRST TIME YOU USE YOUR PHONE EACH DAY? WHEN IS THE LAST TIME YOU USE YOUR PHONE BEFORE BED?

7:30 AM

HOW HAVE YOU SEEN YOUR PHONE USE IMPACT YOUR TIME WITH
FAMILY AND FRIENDS?

HOW DO YOU THINK YOUR PHONE IS NEGATIVELY IMPACTING THE
PERSON YOU ARE BECOMING? HOW DO YOU THINK YOUR PHONE IS
POSITIVELY IMPACTING THE PERSON YOU ARE BECOMING?

WHEN YOU THINK OF YOURSELF A YEAR FROM NOW, WHAT WOULD
YOU LIKE YOUR PHONE USE TO LOOK LIKE?

WHAT ARE THREE CHANGES YOU THINK YOU MIGHT NEED TO MAKE WITH HOW YOU USE YOUR PHONE?

When can I check messages?
morning + after a good
days work.

- Lets get total pick ups a
day ~~to~~ down

"

*Help me realize that there is no
goodness in my phone that is better than
what I can find in You. Help me to use
my phone in a way that allows me to
discover how good You truly are.*

OUR WORKS DO
NOT SAVE US BUT
ARE EXPRESSIONS
OF LOVE, DEVOTION,
AND OBEDIENCE
TO HIM.

Helpful Tips

You are about to begin writing out a plan to set goals to help you change your relationship with your phone and the amount of time you give to it. Remember, our phones are not the problem. The problem is within our hearts (Jeremiah 17:9). This section provides tips to help you brainstorm your plan. However, you should make these changes to your phone use in light of the gospel. We are covered in the righteousness of Jesus if we call Him our Savior. And while we seek to obey and love our heavenly Father, our works do not save us but are expressions of love, devotion, and obedience to Him. By putting your phone in its proper place, you are growing in love for your God.

TIP #1: Keep your phone in a separate charging station away from your nightstand and potentially outside of your room. If you use your phone as your alarm, consider purchasing a separate alarm to keep on your nightstand. This will help you form good morning and nighttime habits. It is good to get a break from your screen. It also allows you to focus on the Lord as you begin and end your day.

TIP #2: Replace the instinct to grab your phone first thing in the morning and before you go to sleep at night. Replace the time you would spend on your phone with other activities you love! What are things that energize you as you begin your day that would also cause you to dwell more on the Lord? What are things that would calm you down at night and give you time to reflect on things that happened during the day? These will be different for each person! Developing your prayer life by reading through and praying the Psalms would be a great idea to use during either one of those times!

TIP #3: Delete each app that you do not use regularly or is stealing too much of your time. Some apps that we have misused do not need to leave our phones forever. We may just need to set some ground rules for how to use them correctly, but some apps are doing nothing to produce in us more love for the Lord. Pray and seek out godly counsel for apps that may need to leave your phone permanently or for a season.

TIP #4: Organize your apps into folders, and make your home screen very empty. Maybe only have three to five apps on it, and let those be apps that help you love the Lord. In those few home screen apps, you could include the ESV Bible app, the Dwell App, and the Podcasts App. This will make your home screen less distracting and also nudge you to be with the Lord as soon as you open your phone.

TIP #5: Consider turning off notifications at a certain time of the day. If you are able, it might be wise to consider turning off notifications altogether. This will keep you from constantly picking up your phone as it dings to remind you of something else you need to do or another message to check.

TIP #6: Consider having daily, weekly, and yearly breaks from your phone. How could you implement some rest time from your device to help you break your attachment to it?

TIP #7: Set a goal for how much non-work-related screen time you want to have each day. Set goals, and enable screen time restrictions, specifically for social media and entertainment screen time. Give the password for these restrictions to someone else so that you cannot disable it. You may feel frustrated the first time your phone does not let you keep scrolling through Instagram and YouTube, but the more you comply with these restrictions, the less you will need those apps.

Now, it is time to brainstorm! Take a few minutes, and write down your top ideas for your plan to redeem your phone time.

WHAT ARE SOME WAYS THAT I CAN REDEEM MY PHONE TIME?

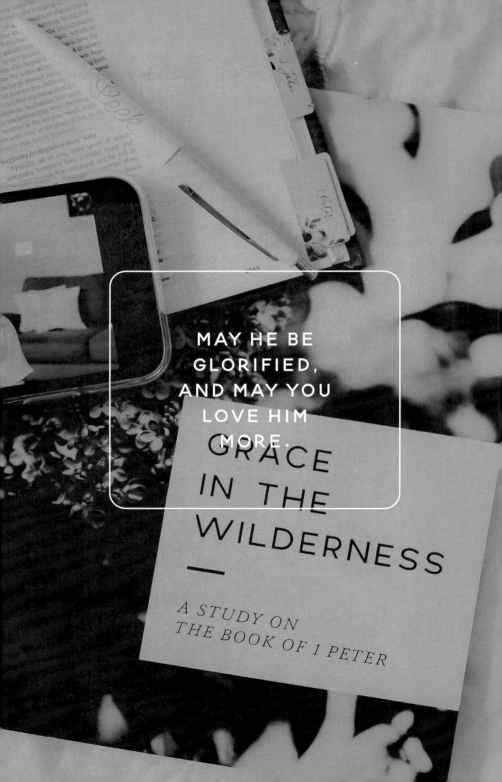

MAY HE BE
GLORIFIED,
AND MAY YOU
LOVE HIM
MORE.

GRACE
IN THE
WILDERNESS
—

A STUDY ON
THE BOOK OF 1 PETER

Make a Plan

It is finally time to fill out the pages at the front of this booklet to create your plan to redeem your phone time! Making this plan will likely use at least a day of this challenge. It would be wise to allow yourself to start now and take the next two days of Part 2 to complete it. Once you finish Part 2, you will begin implementing your plan.

The following are several passages from God's Word to encourage you in your endeavor. May He be glorified, and may you love Him more!

PSALM 16

Protect me, God, for I take refuge in you.
I said to the Lord, "You are my Lord;
I have nothing good besides you."
As for the holy people who are in the land,
they are the noble ones.
All my delight is in them.
The sorrows of those who take another god
for themselves will multiply;
I will not pour out their drink offerings of blood,
and I will not speak their names with my lips.

Lord, you are my portion
and my cup of blessing;
you hold my future.
The boundary lines have fallen for me
in pleasant places;
indeed, I have a beautiful inheritance.

I will bless the Lord who counsels me—
even at night when my thoughts trouble me.
I always let the Lord guide me.
Because he is at my right hand,
I will not be shaken.

Therefore my heart is glad
and my whole being rejoices;
my body also rests securely.
For you will not abandon me to Sheol;
you will not allow your faithful one to see decay.
You reveal the path of life to me;
in your presence is abundant joy;
at your right hand are eternal pleasures.

2 CORINTHIANS 3:18

We all, with unveiled faces, are looking as in a mirror at the glory
of the Lord and are being transformed into the same image from
glory to glory; this is from the Lord who is the Spirit.

1 PETER 2:13-25

Submit to every human authority because of the Lord, whether to
the emperor as the supreme authority or to governors as those sent
out by him to punish those who do what is evil and to praise those
who do what is good. For it is God's will that you silence the
ignorance of foolish people by doing good. Submit as free people,
not using your freedom as a cover-up for evil, but as God's slaves.
Honor everyone. Love the brothers and sisters. Fear God. Honor
the emperor.

Household slaves, submit to your masters with all reverence not
only to the good and gentle ones but also to the cruel. For it brings
favor if, because of a consciousness of God, someone endures grief
from suffering unjustly. For what credit is there if when you do
wrong and are beaten, you endure it? But when you do what is
good and suffer, if you endure it, this brings favor with God.

For you were called to this, because Christ also suffered for you, leaving you an example, that you should follow in his steps. He did not commit sin, and no deceit was found in his mouth; when he was insulted, he did not insult in return; when he suffered, he did not threaten but entrusted himself to the one who judges justly. He himself bore our sins in his body on the tree; so that, having died to sins, we might live for righteousness. By his wounds you have been healed. For you were like sheep going astray, but you have now returned to the Shepherd and Overseer of your souls.

NOTES

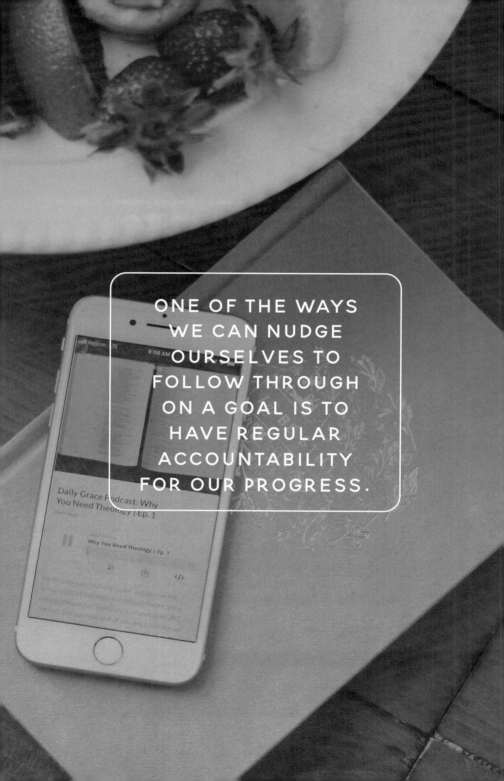

ONE OF THE WAYS
WE CAN NUDGE
OURSELVES TO
FOLLOW THROUGH
ON A GOAL IS TO
HAVE REGULAR
ACCOUNTABILITY
FOR OUR PROGRESS.

Find Accountability

When you embark on any kind of life change, it is probably wise to tell someone. Whether you like it or not, because our phones can become so addictive, modifying the way we use them does not necessarily come naturally on the first day. And it will probably not be perfect the second or third day either. You may feel like giving up when you repeat an unhealthy phone habit or do not follow your plan as well as you would have liked. At the end of the day, we are responsible for the choices and decisions we make with the time and resources we have. However, we can make wise choices that will help us make good decisions in the future. We do this by anticipating our weaknesses and putting up safeguards that nudge us in the right direction. One of the ways we can nudge ourselves to follow through on a goal is to have regular accountability for our progress.

When choosing someone to hold you accountable for your new phone habits, remember that this person is a gift to you. This person is helping you be more intentional with the way that you spend time on your phone, and should probably be someone you see face to face on a regular basis. Having someone text you each time to hold you accountable is may not be the wisest choice since you will be trying to avoid unnecessary screen time. It would also be very easy to twist the truth since you do not have to look someone in the eyes to answer their questions directly.

When you ask someone to hold you accountable, explain why you are doing this challenge and how many days he or she should ask you about it. The challenge is to follow your plan for thirty days. That means the two of you should set a goal to have thirty little conversations. Ask your friend, roommate, or husband if this is something he or she can commit to doing, and tell the person you understand if it is not. If this person does not have time to ask you every day, it may not be as helpful for you. If the person you ask tells you "yes," show him or her the front pages of this book where you have either started or completed your plan. It might be a good idea to have your accountability partner take pictures of your goals to know what to ask you about from day to day. Decide on a time when this person will ask you every day about your phone habits, and consider pairing this time with another thing you already do together so that it comes about naturally. Maybe this person could join in the challenge with you, which could be the perfect encouragement for you both.

Sanctification and growth in discipline do not come without some struggle, but in it, you will always discover more freedom! Finding the right people to help you along the way is a crucial step in the process!

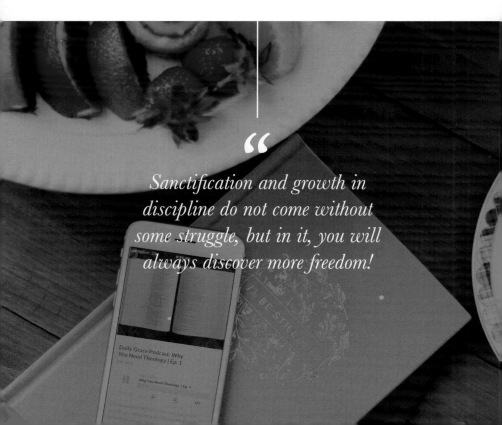

Sanctification and growth in discipline do not come without some struggle, but in it, you will always discover more freedom!

WRITE DOWN THE NAME OF THE PERSON WHO WILL BE YOUR FREEDOM PARTNER BELOW.

EXPLAIN WHY YOU CHOSE THIS PERSON AND WHEN YOU WILL BE HAVING YOUR CONVERSATIONS EACH DAY.

WRITE A LETTER OF GRATITUDE TO YOUR ACCOUNTABILITY PARTNER FOR INVESTING THIS TIME INTO HELPING YOU GROW IN SELF-CONTROL AND LOVE FOR THE LORD.

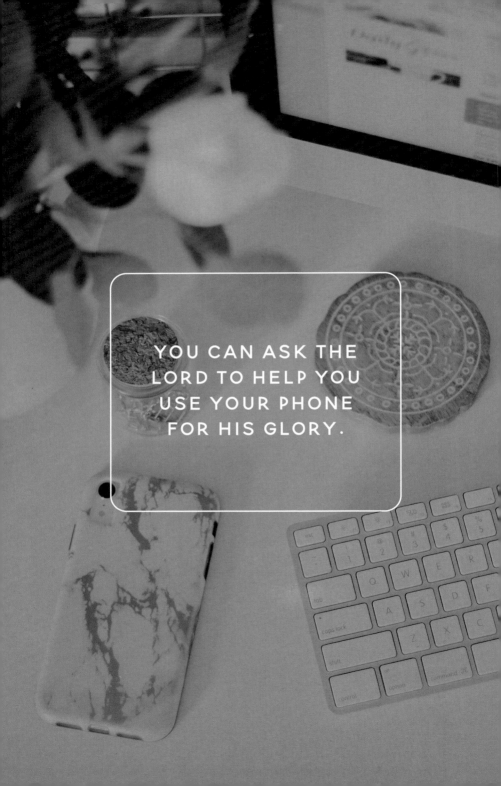

YOU CAN ASK THE LORD TO HELP YOU USE YOUR PHONE FOR HIS GLORY.

Know Your Why

Tomorrow is the day you begin! You have already completed so much in preparation for this challenge. You have also allowed yourself ample time to reflect on your habits. Well done! These are not easy things to do, and self-examination can be difficult, but the end reward of exercising self-control over your phone will be well worth your efforts. And as you go through this challenge, it will be profitable to think about that end reward—your motivator for ordering this book in the first place. It is your why.

Why are you doing this challenge? Here are some possible "whys":

To love your time in the Word of God

To treasure your family

To learn how to rest well but also be productive

To increase your ability to concentrate on reading and focus on conversations around you

To find your affirmation in the Lord and not in the opinions of others

To find your peace in God

To be comfortable in stillness

To live an undistracted life where you focus on the mission at hand—that others may know Jesus through how you live your life

Your device cannot control you. The Word of God will be your guide, and you will be able to use your phone in a way that honors the Lord and lets you love Him and others all the more. Once you know your "why," you can turn back to it on the most challenging days. You can ask the Lord to help you use your phone for His glory, and He will help you, for this pursuit honors Him.

Devices are not going away. They will only get more technologically advanced, which will in turn bring more distraction. We must learn to exercise discipline in our use of them. They can either be a great hindrance to us or an enormous blessing. Do we want our lives characterized by what we did with time spent on our phones or how much time we spent growing in understanding of God's Word and were present with our family and friends? Which one is the most important to you? What is your "why"? Identify it, and begin!

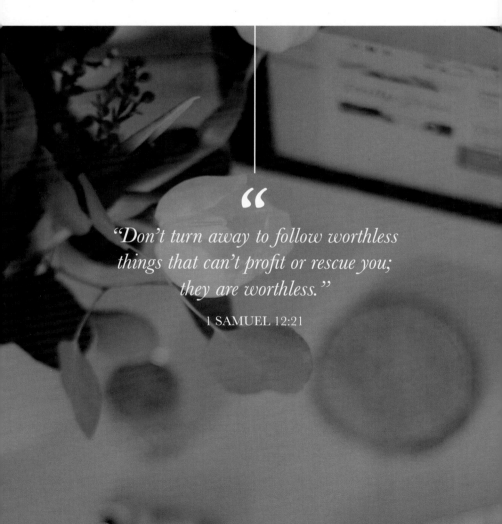

"
"Don't turn away to follow worthless things that can't profit or rescue you; they are worthless."

1 SAMUEL 12:21

TURN TO THE FRONT OF THE BOOKLET, AND FILL OUT THE PAGE THAT IS DESIGNATED FOR YOUR "WHY." REVIEW YOUR "WHY" PAGE OFTEN THROUGHOUT THIS CHALLENGE SO THAT YOU CAN REMEMBER WHY YOU ARE MAKING THESE CHANGES. THERE WILL BE HARD DAYS, SO REMIND YOURSELF WHY YOU BEGAN THIS CHALLENGE.

READ EPHESIANS 3:14-21, AND USE IT AS A PRAYER TO THE LORD AS YOU CLOSE OUT YOUR TIME TODAY.

Truths to REMEMBER

HIS PRESENCE IS WHERE THERE IS JOY FOREVERMORE.

Remember the Better Thing

Whether you are reading this at the beginning of the day or before you go to sleep, congratulations on completing the first day of the challenge to redeem your phone time! If you are reading this in the morning, remember that the Lord is your strength, and you can call out to Him every moment of the day. If you are reading this in the evening, reflect on your first day of the challenge. Did you follow through with your daily goals? If not, what stopped you? How will you try and make a different decision tomorrow?

As you reflect, remember that all progress is never perfect. The goal of this challenge is not to accomplish thirty days of perfectly following all the rules you made for yourself. The goal is to grow in self-control with your phone so that rather than being enslaved to it, you can use it as a tool to love the Lord more. Today may have been full of urges to check your notifications or the nagging temptations to scroll mindlessly through social media feeds during lunchtime, and that is okay. Small acts of faithfulness each day are the key to breaking a bad habit. Celebrate the victories from today, and reflect on the mistakes. Use the victories to encourage you to persevere tomorrow, and let the mistakes be healthy reminders that you are completely dependent on the Lord.

Above all, remember that the Lord is so much greater than what our phones have to offer. Loving God and being in His presence is better than anything you will find on your phone. His presence is where there is joy forevermore. He offers us abundant life. He gives us rest for our souls. Yet even after God saves us, we still look for satisfaction in the wrong things. Why? Because we are prone to forget our God, even though He never forgets us.

So we have to say to ourselves, "God is better." We need to hear it aloud as we are tempted to believe something else could give us something better than what the Lord can give us—Himself.

As you reflect on today's reading, remember these truths about the Lord, and let them be gentle nudges to your heart and mind as you seek to put your phone in its proper place. He is worthy of all our affection.

The Lord's presence is always available to me.

The Lord has known me before the foundation of the world, and He loved me even when I did not love Him in return.

The Lord has adopted me into His family. I can depend fully on Him because He is my perfect, gracious heavenly Father.

I will someday be in heaven with the Lord, and I will not be concerned about my phone, for I will have much greater things to dwell on and experience than anything my phone can give.

Remember that the Lord is so much greater than what our phones have to offer.

WRITE OUT ON A NOTECARD THE WORDS, "HE IS BETTER."
PLACE THE NOTECARD SOMEWHERE YOU WILL SEE IT
THROUGHOUT THE DAY, AND WHENEVER YOU SEE IT,
READ IT ALOUD.

READ PHILIPPIANS 4:19. LIST OUT FIVE WAYS THAT THE
RICHES OF GOD FULFILL ALL YOUR NEEDS IN A WAY YOUR
PHONE NEVER COULD.

READ ZEPHANIAH 3:17. HOW DOES KNOWING THAT THE LORD
IS IN YOUR MIDST AND HIS STEADFAST LOVE IS WHOLLY YOURS
ENCOURAGE YOU TO CONTINUE IN THIS CHALLENGE?

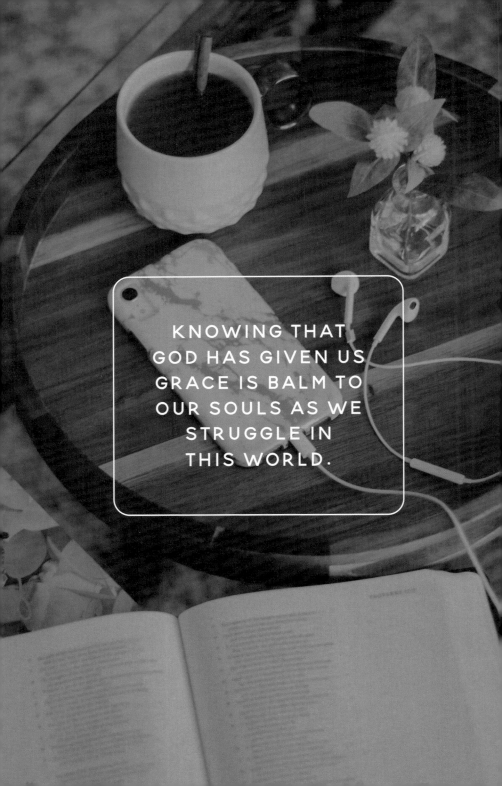

KNOWING THAT
GOD HAS GIVEN US
GRACE IS BALM TO
OUR SOULS AS WE
STRUGGLE IN
THIS WORLD.

Remember He Gives More Grace

The grace of God is defined as "the free and unmerited favor of God, as manifested in the salvation of sinners and the bestowal of blessings." As you begin the second day of your challenge, pause for a moment, and consider the grace God has bestowed upon you. It is completely free; you did nothing to earn it. You have favor with the King of kings, and He has given you salvation and every spiritual blessing because of the work of Christ (Ephesians 1:3).

Knowing that God has given us grace is balm to our souls as we struggle in this world. Today is another opportunity to rest in that grace of God as you choose to spend less time on your phone and more time intentionally living for His glory. And you are making these decisions because of God's grace.

Think of what God's grace has allowed for you up to this moment in your life. You were born into the world covered in sin, and God opened your eyes to the truth of the gospel. He allowed you to see who He is and brought you from death to life. And not only does He give you true and abundant life here on earth, but He also promises you eternal life with Him when you die. Death is not the end for you because of His grace. While you live in this world, God reveals Himself to you more each day and gives you opportunities to see Him in everything around you. Creation reveals Him to you—the nature outside your window and your friends and family—and He reveals Himself to you through His. James 4:4-8 says this:

> You adulterous people! Don't you know that friendship with the world is hostility toward God? So whoever wants to be the friend of the world becomes the enemy of God. Or do you think it's without reason that the Scripture says:

The spirit he made to dwell in us envies intensely? But he gives greater grace. Therefore he says: God resists the proud, but gives grace to the humble. Therefore, submit to God. Resist the devil, and he will flee from you. Draw near to God, and he will draw near to you.

The world covets our focus and attention, therefore, we must intentionally choose to look to the Lord, and He gives us the grace to do so! When we are humble in heart and draw near to Him, He will draw near to us. He desires that we will cry out to Him and depend on Him alone. Are you struggling with love for the world by desiring your phone more than the Lord? Call out to Him, and draw near to Him in His Word! He will come near to you.

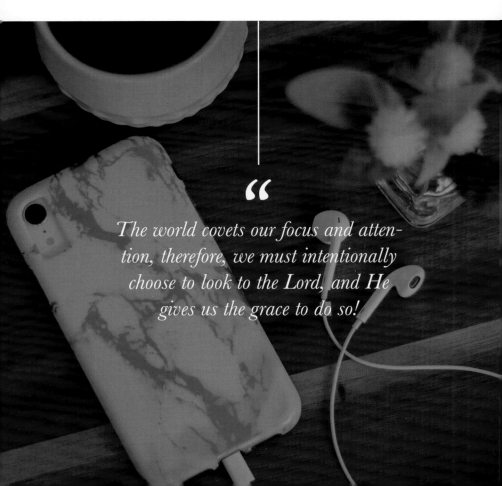

The world covets our focus and attention, therefore, we must intentionally choose to look to the Lord, and He gives us the grace to do so!

WHAT ARE THREE SPECIFIC WAYS THE LORD HAS SHOWN
GRACE TO YOU? (WHAT BLESSINGS HAVE YOU RECEIVED
IN YOUR LIFE THAT YOU DO NOT DESERVE?)

HOW DOES KNOWING THAT YOU WORK OUT OF GOD'S GRACE
RATHER THAN YOUR OWN STRENGTH ENCOURAGE YOU?

HOW CAN YOU DRAW NEAR TO GOD TODAY IN THIS
PHONE CHALLENGE?

THE LORD USES
QUIET MOMENTS TO
DRAW US TO HIM-
SELF AND REFOCUS
OUR HEARTS.

Remember to Be Still

As smartphones became a part of the fabric of our society, there was a perpetual loss of quiet moments. Before smartphones, when we had to stand in line at the store and wait for our turn to check out, we would look around or think to ourselves while the cashier helped whoever was in front of us, reflecting on our day or thinking about the next thing we had to do. Waiting in line at drive-thrus meant you were probably listening to the radio or chatting with a friend in the car. We could go on and on, but what is important to realize is that we have many opportunities for quiet moments, and many times, the Lord uses those quiet moments to draw us to Himself and refocus our hearts. Even if every smartphone suddenly vanished, human beings would still find a way to fill these quiet moments, but the simple truth is that our devices make it relatively easy to do so.

The disciples knew very well that Jesus took time to be away with His heavenly Father. Many of His days were consumed with meeting the physical and spiritual needs of the people He met. Jesus did not have much time alone as He taught the disciples and the crowds who followed Him, so He habitually withdrew to be alone and pray. If Jesus practiced this discipline, it would be wise of us to follow His example.

So today, while you persist in having your phone in its proper place and spending time away from it, why not practice being still? Pause today with the Lord without any distractions, and enjoy Him. Sitting in silence and being alone can seem frightening or even boring. But, these moments of stillness can lead to a deeper awareness of the Lord's presence, and this awareness of His presence will affect every aspect of your day. We need to be still and remember that He is God, and He is with us. It is also in silence and solitude that we can make room for other spiritual disciplines like Bible study, meditation, and prayer. Limiting your time on your phone allows you to practice these disciplines, and it also gives you time to ask the Lord to quiet your heart and calm your soul. We find things to worry about every day, but silence in the Lord's presence puts our worries in the right place and gives us back some quiet moments.

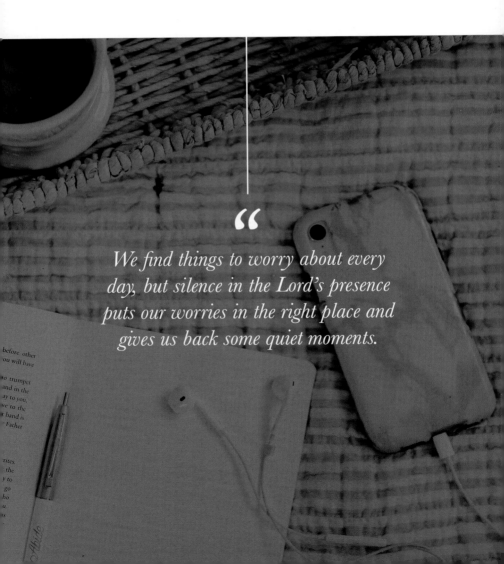

We find things to worry about every day, but silence in the Lord's presence puts our worries in the right place and gives us back some quiet moments.

TAKE FIVE MINUTES TO BE SILENT BEFORE THE LORD. USING YOUR PHONE OR A COMPUTER, PLAY YOUR FAVORITE HYMN. SET YOUR DEVICE ASIDE OR ACROSS THE ROOM AS THE HYMN PLAYS, AND CONSIDER GOD'S CHARACTER AS YOU FOCUS ON THE LYRICS. IF YOU DO NOT HAVE A FAVORITE HYMN OR ARE HAVING TROUBLE THINKING OF ONE, A FEW POSSIBLE OPTIONS ARE "HOLY, HOLY, HOLY," "JUST AS I AM," AND "I NEED THEE EVERY HOUR."

READ THE FOLLOWING VERSES IN YOUR BIBLE REGARDING SILENCE AND SOLITUDE, AND ASK THE LORD HOW YOU CAN MAKE THIS PRACTICE A PART OF YOUR LIFE: PSALM 62, ISAIAH 30:15, LAMENTATIONS 3:25-28, AND MARK 6:31.

HOW HAS YOUR PHONE STOLEN SOME OF YOUR QUIET MOMENTS? WHAT PART OF YOUR PLAN IS HELPING YOU REGAIN SOME OF THOSE MOMENTS?

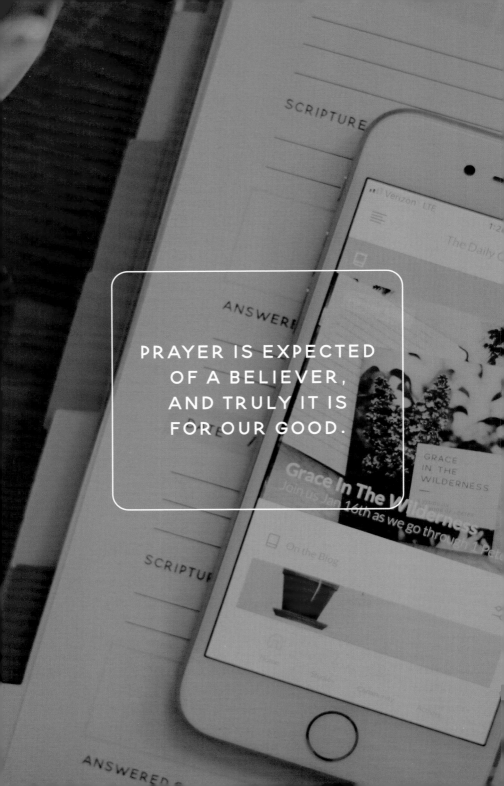

PRAYER IS EXPECTED
OF A BELIEVER,
AND TRULY IT IS
FOR OUR GOOD.

Remember to Pray

Our phones allow us to communicate throughout the day. We can talk to practically anyone, and it does not matter if that person is across the world from us or in the next room. There seems to be no limit on who we can reach, as long as a device is in our hands. These devices sometimes cause us to forget that we are not omnipresent like the Lord—we cannot be in multiple places at once. And by filling our time communicating with person after person, we can also forget to commune with our heavenly Father, the One we need most. As we seek to be self-controlled with our devices, there are pockets of time when it is tempting to pick up our phones and check notifications and messages, but we can fill this time and train our minds to turn to our Father instead.

When Jesus teaches His disciples how to pray, He does not instruct them that "if" they will pray, but "when" they will pray (Luke 11:2). Prayer is expected of a believer, and truly it is for our good. Jesus tells us in John 15:5, "you can do nothing without me." If there is an absence of prayer in our lives, it likely reveals a misunderstanding of our need for the Lord and His desire to respond to His children's requests (Matthew 7:7-8). Our phones cannot fulfill our deepest longings and needs. They can most certainly help us love the Lord when we learn how to use them well, but our souls need our Father, and prayer is the avenue through which we come into His presence.

We unintentionally create unhealthy rhythms with our phones, so intentionally creating a healthy rhythm of prayer can certainly feel challenging at first, but we must remind ourselves what prayer is. Prayer is where we can come before the Lord, the King of kings, the Creator of the world, our dearest friend, and speak to Him, and He speaks to us as we pray through His Word.

Prayer provides rest for our souls, and it grounds us in the truth that life on earth is fleeting, but life with our Father in heaven is eternal. Prayer gives us a picture of the life that is coming—one where we will dwell in the courts of the Lord forever.

So as you put away your phone and remember to pray, here are some ideas to get you started!

Find a blank journal where you can write out your prayers to the Lord. Find your favorite pens, highlighters, and even stickers. Turn on some quiet worship music, and make the pages beautiful as you worship your Father above. Do not be afraid of being honest in this journal. The Lord loves when we come before Him with all of our questions, fears, and even frustrations.

As you clean your house or complete different tasks, pair a task with a person or situation to pray for. You could pair emptying the dishwasher with praying aloud for a dear friend or spouse. You could pair a silent car ride with praying for whatever is lying heavy on your heart. The more you practice pairing in this way, the more you will notice an inclination toward prayer.

Open your Bible to the book of Psalms, and use a few of them to help guide you as you walk through prayer. Use the language of the Psalms to help you speak to the Lord and keep you from distraction. Feel free to pray about the circumstances of your life by using the language of the text.

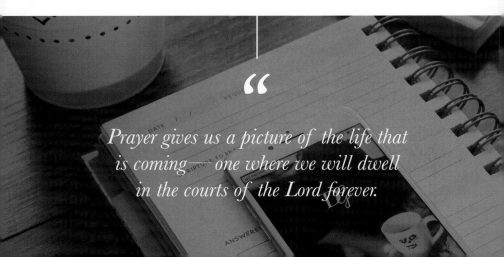

"

Prayer gives us a picture of the life that is coming—one where we will dwell in the courts of the Lord forever.

Day Fourteen Questions

HOW HAS YOUR PHONE ADDED TO OR HINDERED YOUR PRAYER LIFE?

HOW WOULD YOU LIKE YOUR PRAYER LIFE TO LOOK DIFFERENT FROM WHAT IT IS NOW?

WHAT ARE SOME THOUGHTS OR IDEAS TO HELP YOU GET STARTED USING CONSISTENT RHYTHMS OF PRAYER? WHEN WILL YOU SET ASIDE TIME TODAY TO PRAY?

GOD HAS GIVEN
HUMANITY A NEED
FOR A RHYTHM
OF REST.

Remember to Rest

Our smartphones are centers of constant activity. They always have something else for us to look at, read, or dig into. After a long day of working or running errands, sometimes nothing sounds better than to throw ourselves on the couch and scroll for a while. We tell ourselves we will get on with our next task in five minutes as we watch one funny video after another, but five minutes slowly turns into an hour, and now we are behind on something or busy once again, and for some reason, we feel just as tired.

When we never give ourselves breaks from our phones, our minds can become just like them. Constantly turning, worrying, and thinking about hundreds of different things, never silent or at rest. And when rest is absent in our lives, we will often notice that we become easily irritable and overwhelmed.

God has given humanity a need for a rhythm of rest, which is why we see Him modeling rest to us after He finished His week of creation (Genesis 2:2). The Lord would later command the people of Israel to imitate Him in resting by keeping the Sabbath holy. They would remember the rest of the Lord that began in the garden, and this rest would point them to the future rest they would have with the Lord once again. When Jesus spoke about the Sabbath, He revolutionized the way the Israelites saw it by declaring Himself, "Lord of the Sabbath" (Matthew 12:8). He was the rest for whom the people had been waiting. Jesus brings us back into fellowship with God, and one day we will physically fellowship with God again in eternity as Adam and Eve did in the garden (Revelation 22:1-5).

So while the Lord no longer requires us to practice all of the Sabbath laws, we still need to rest and set aside a portion of time each week to rest intentionally with the Lord and our families. Doing so points us toward the eternal rest we will one day have in heaven. This is a perfect time to put away our phones for a while and experience true rest and enjoy family and friends. We put our phones away, and we remember the things that matter in light of eternity. Here are a couple of ideas for using this time you set aside:

Have everyone in your family work on preparing a special meal together. Play your favorite music and sing together as you make it. If you have children who cannot help make the meal, let them choose a few read-aloud stories to read through together during dinner.

Choose a neighbor, elderly church member, or friend to bless with a home-made treat and letters from your family. Surprise this person with it, and see how he or she is doing.

"
We put our phones away, and we remember the things that matter in light of eternity.

HAVE YOU NOTICED AN ABSENCE OF REST IN YOUR LIFE? WHAT CONTRIBUTES MOST TO THIS?

DO YOU THINK THERE IS A DAY OR PERIOD OF TIME YOU COULD SET ASIDE EACH WEEK TO BE AWAY FROM YOUR PHONE AND SIMPLY REST? (DINNERTIME ON SATURDAY TO DINNERTIME ON SUNDAY IS A COMMON PRACTICE FOR MANY!)

HOW DOES THINKING ABOUT OUR ETERNAL REST WITH GOD HELP US CARRY ON TODAY? HOW DOES IT HELP US PUT OUR PHONES IN THEIR PROPER PLACE?

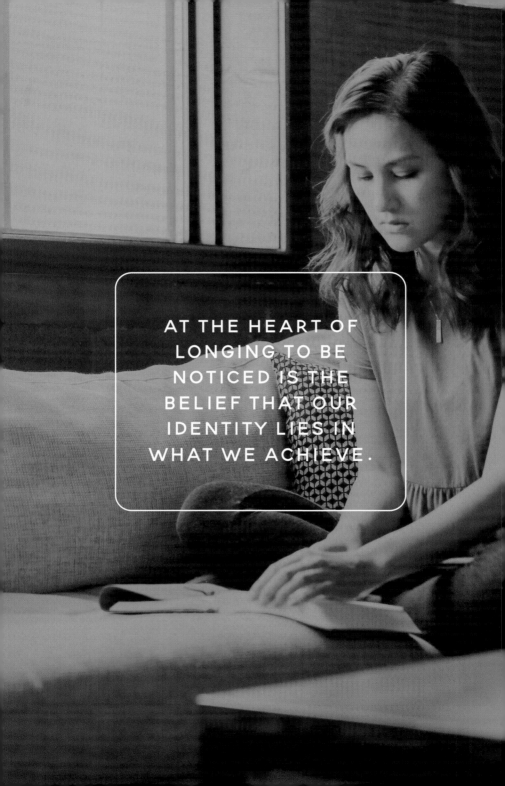

AT THE HEART OF
LONGING TO BE
NOTICED IS THE
BELIEF THAT OUR
IDENTITY LIES IN
WHAT WE ACHIEVE.

Remember to Live a Quiet Life

What would it be like to live hidden away from the world? In an era when most people yearn for a platform with a following and have the resources to gain one, living a hidden life may seem undesirable or even foolish. At the heart of the longing to be noticed is often the belief that our identity lies in what we achieve, what people think of us, and who knows our name. Our phones give us the power to show people parts of who we are and be "known" by the world, but the depth to which people can know us through our screens only goes so far. And the amount of time and energy we put into our online interactions can leave us anxious and emotionally depleted, for our desire to be known can never be completely satisfied in our phones.

Paul tells us in 1 Thessalonians 4:10b-12: "But we encourage you, brothers and sisters, to [love one another] even more, to seek to lead a quiet life, to mind your own business, and to work with your own hands, as we commanded you, so that you may behave properly in the presence of outsiders and not be dependent on anyone." Here, Paul is explaining to the Thessalonians how to walk in spiritual maturity. Instead of esteeming themselves, they were called to love others and live quietly. Instead of trifling in the affairs of others, they were to mind their own business and faithfully work unto the Lord. By growing in these practices, they would be able to model lives patterned after Jesus, and they would move on from spiritual milk to solid food (1 Corinthians 3:1-2).

When we are focused only on being recognized by the world and how we appear through our screens, we stunt our growth and maturity in Christ. We forsake the beauty of living quietly, and we forget that the Lord has always known us. He sees every moment of our days, and He knows all of our thoughts and feelings. While it is not wrong to share our thoughts and special moments on social media, we can relish the fact that the King of kings sees everything about us and loves us. We can be satisfied with living less for the eyes of the world and more for the eyes of the Lord. And by living more unto Him and not for our screens, we will experience a richness and depth of relationships in our homes, communities, and churches that simply cannot happen through our phones. Living quietly does not mean living in solitude but being faithful to the life God has given you. Let us put our phones in their proper place and enjoy the abundance God has so graciously given us.

We can be satisfied with living less for the eyes of the world and more for the eyes of the Lord.

WHAT ARE WAYS YOU TRY TO BE NOTICED BY THE WORLD? HOW HAS THIS EXHAUSTED OR HURT YOU?

WHEN YOU HEAR OF HIDDEN LIFE IN GOD, WHO IS A PERSON THAT EXEMPLIFIES THIS TO YOU? WHAT WOULD YOU LIKE TO IMITATE ABOUT THAT PERSON?

READ PSALM 139. HOW DOES THIS PSALM ENCOURAGE YOU NOT TO BE CONCERNED WITH THE THOUGHTS OF OTHERS?

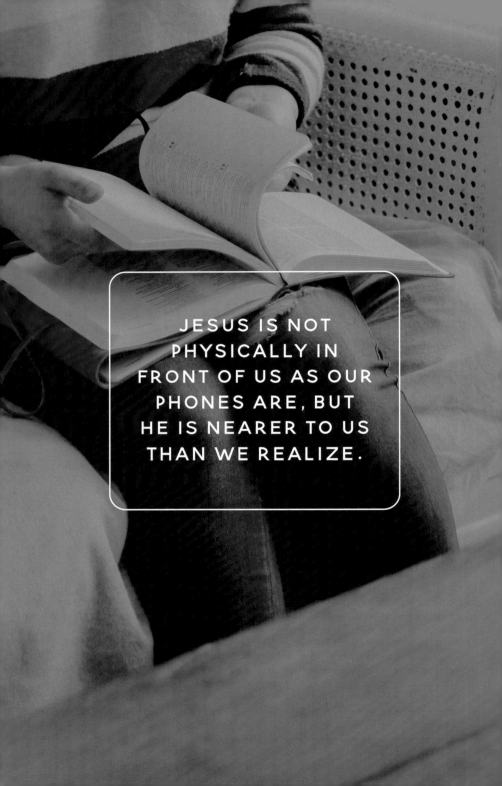

JESUS IS NOT
PHYSICALLY IN
FRONT OF US AS OUR
PHONES ARE, BUT
HE IS NEARER TO US
THAN WE REALIZE.

Remember to Abide

One of the most encouraging passages in Scripture is found in John 15:4-5 when Jesus says to His disciples, "Abide in me, and I in you. As the branch cannot bear fruit by itself, unless it abides in the vine, neither can you, unless you abide in me. I am the vine; you are the branches. Whoever abides in me and I in him, he it is that bears much fruit, for apart from me you can do nothing" (ESV).

The Greek word that Jesus uses for "abide" also means "to remain" and "to continue to be present." How funny it is that in our technological age, our devices are made to keep our attention constantly. Most of us have no problem remaining on our phones or being technologically present, but it can be difficult to remember to remain in Jesus. Jesus is not physically in front of us as our phones are, but He is nearer to us than we realize (Matthew 28:20), for His Spirit is within us (Romans 8:11).

But what does it even mean to remain in Him? How can understanding this truth of the Christian life help us? While we may be tempted to throw in the towel while trying to abide in Christ rather than our phones, we need to understand that abiding in Jesus is not something we can naturally do on our own. Abiding in Him is a gift He has given to us. When we are given new hearts by the Lord and faith from Him to accept Jesus as our Savior, we are covered in Christ's righteousness and acquitted from our sins. Because we are covered in Christ's righteousness, we experience union with Him. This union never ceases, as even right now, we are united to Christ. This means that we have access to Him and who He is every moment of the day. We can rely on Him for strength as we put our phones away and pick up our Bibles instead. We can depend on Him to give us love for others as we communicate on our devices. And we can rely on Him for peace as we see troubling news announcements on our social media feeds.

On our own, we cannot do any of this. Trying to use our phones to glorify God would be impossible, but we are united with Jesus. We have the help of our Savior. This union with Jesus will never be interrupted, but our remembrance to abide in Him can be. So we must remember that our lives are an outflow of our union with Jesus, and we must stay near to Him. The more we learn to remain in Jesus, the more we will put our phones in their proper place as we learn to use them in better ways.

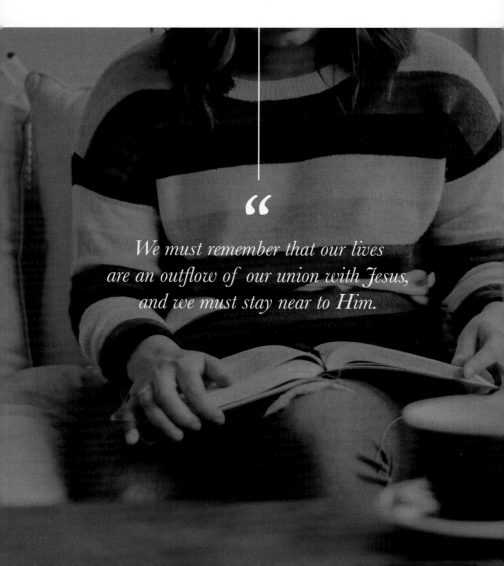

"

We must remember that our lives are an outflow of our union with Jesus, and we must stay near to Him.

WHAT IS A PHRASE YOU CAN SAY TO YOURSELF THROUGHOUT THE DAY THAT HELPS YOU REMEMBER THAT YOU ARE UNITED WITH CHRIST AND NEED TO REMAIN IN HIM? JESUS SAYS IN JOHN 15:4, "REMAIN IN ME, AND I IN YOU." WHERE CAN YOU POST THIS PIECE OF SCRIPTURE TO HELP YOU REMEMBER IT THROUGHOUT THE DAY?

IF WE ARE NOT ABIDING IN CHRIST, IN WHAT OTHER SORTS OF THINGS DO WE END UP ABIDING? HOW CAN THESE THINGS HURT US?

READ AND MEDITATE ON JOHN 15 AND 1 JOHN 4:15. HOW DOES KNOWING THAT YOU HAVE BEEN GIVEN THE GIFT OF ABIDING IN CHRIST CHANGE HOW YOU LIVE? HOW CAN YOU VIEW YOUR DAY DIFFERENTLY IN LIGHT OF THIS TRUTH?

DWELLING ON SCRIPTURE WILL DO SO MUCH MORE FOR OUR MINDS THAN OUR PHONES CAN.

Remember to Dwell

Scrolling on our phones has become one of our favorite pastimes. It is a learned habit since we are not born with an awareness of technology, and it is a recent development in our culture with the advancement of smartphones. Most of us would not know what to do with ourselves if this habit did not occupy some part of our time during the day. We linger over our phones and absorb what they give us, and the result of this is filling our minds with everything we see on them. Not everything on our phones is useless. We can learn wonderful, helpful information through our devices. Still, when our minds linger on them instead of the Word of God, we are essentially choosing to study a collection of doodles instead of an exquisite painting.

Dwelling on Scripture—sitting with it, studying it, memorizing it, and meditating on it—will do so much more for our minds than our phones can. Meditating on Scripture promises to transform our minds, and the life of a righteous person is marked by this practice as well (Psalm 1). When we dwell on the things of this world, our minds will be shaped by them, sometimes casing anxiety or depression. There is much more of the world for us to dwell on in our day and age, and with ongoing phone addictions, we do just that. However, when we meditate and dwell on the things of God, we see different outcomes:

> We become careful and aware to do what is written in God's Word (Joshua 1:8).

> We will experience blessing from God's hand (Joshua 1:8).

> We will bear healthy fruit (Psalm 1:3).

> We will be at peace in times of trouble (John 14:27).

We will think of the Lord more often through the day and night (Psalm 1:2).

We will remember our union with Christ and be encouraged that we operate out of His strength (John 15:5).

Try as they might, our phones cannot promise any of these outcomes. Only time spent in the Word of God can. So as you go throughout your day, try to follow the plan for your phone you created for yourself. I also recommend having a passage of Scripture readily available for you to think on and absorb throughout the day. Reading this Scripture is not a "one and done" thing. This is reading a verse or passage and thinking carefully about what it means. You will be reading it again and again, and it will change you in a way that your smartphone cannot.

"

When we meditate and dwell on the things of God, we see different outcomes.

WHAT DO YOU TEND TO DWELL ON MOST DURING THE DAY?

HOW COULD YOU KEEP A PASSAGE OF SCRIPTURE NEAR TO MEDITATE ON? WHAT PASSAGES WOULD YOU LIKE TO KEEP CLOSE?

HOW IS MEDITATION ON SCRIPTURE DIFFERENT FROM MEDITATION ON THE WORLD?

WHAT IF WE ASKED
THE LORD TO MAKE
US CONTENT IN
HIM AND OPEN OUR
EYES TO SEE ALL OF
THE WAYS HE HAS
BLESSED US?

Remember to Slow Down

Life is already moving quickly, but it can move even faster when we are on our phones. We are always posting, scrolling, sharing, and updating. We can find new stories and things to read with just a few taps of our fingers. Social media feeds into this quickness of life. The people we follow post one new life event and then another and another. While these posts are exciting and fun to see, they remind us that this life does not slow down. It keeps going and going without waiting for us to keep up, and we are all quickly headed toward eternity.

Misusing our devices and spending too much time on them can cause us to forget to slow down since slowing down is the opposite of what our phones were designed to encourage us to do. The Lord has given us things to enjoy right in front of us. There are so many blessings for which to be grateful, and nothing on our phones can replace or outshine them. Being more present virtually than in our present day-to-day lives can create a lack of contentment within us. As we see everything everyone else is doing or experiencing, we can often develop feelings of jealousy and fear. We desire the things that others have, and we worry that we will never be satisfied.

What if we just put our phones away in a drawer for a few hours or even days and asked the Lord to make us content in Him and open our eyes to see all of the ways He has blessed us? We would not be able to list them all!

Slowing down is something we should regularly remember to do because we are human and prone to forget. But if we create certain habits to help us pause, it will become a natural part of our lives. Here are a few ideas to get you started as you put your phone away and slow down.

Go outside each day, and pray to the Lord. Ask Him to help you in your day and to open your eyes to see the ways He is working in it.

Sit down in silence, and take a few minutes to just be still. Think about what the best moments of your day have been so far. Think about what has been difficult. Then decide how you can glorify God with the remaining moments of your day.

Create a gratitude list in a visible spot in your house. Invite everyone in your home to participate in adding items to the list.

Journal about your day. If journaling intimidates you, have a set of three or four questions that you answer each day. Journaling is a great reflective practice that helps you keep track of how you are growing or learning. It forces you to put your thoughts into words.

If you have never made a conscious effort to slow down, realize that it may feel difficult and unnatural, but doing so offers priceless rewards!

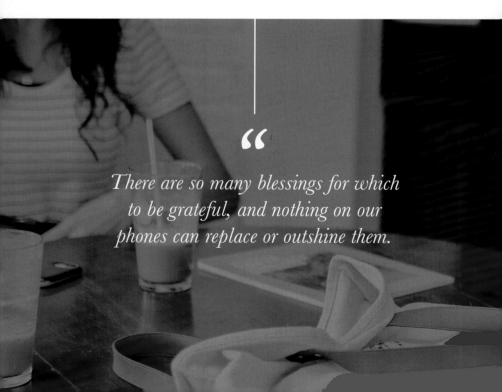

There are so many blessings for which to be grateful, and nothing on our phones can replace or outshine them.

HOW DID JESUS MODEL A "SLOWED DOWN" LIFE FOR US?
(READ ONE ACCOUNT OF JESUS IN MARK 5:25-34 WHEN HE
TOOK TIME TO SPEAK TO A WOMAN WHO DESIRED HEALING)

HOW DOES LIVING IN A FAST-PACED WORLD WEAR ON YOU?

WHAT IS ONE THING YOU WANT TO DO TO SLOW DOWN?

EVEN THOUGH WE
CANNOT SEE HIM,
IT DOES NOT MAKE
HIS PRESENCE ANY
LESS MEANINGFUL.

Remember His Presence

Sometimes it is easy for us to forget that there is so much more going on around us than we realize. In this world, it is easy to think only about what is physically in front of us, but the unseen things around us are just as real. The Lord is always with us, and even though we cannot see Him, it does not make His presence any less meaningful than the presence of other people we see frequently.

Big tech companies actively try to create peer-to-peer interaction and community in online environments. Even though online friendships can be rich and meaningful, these people are often not present with us as we live out our lives. But the Lord—our great Creator, Redeemer, and Friend—is. He sees everything that happens in our lives—all of the moments we want to hide from social media and all of the memories we decide to post. He is sovereign over all of our steps, and yet we live as though the people across our screen are more real than He is.

Oh, how different our lives would be if we sought to think about His presence more and remember that He was with us. Would we always reach for our phones when we have a moment to spare, or would we linger with Him in the quiet, thinking about who He is and how knowing His identity changes our day? Remembering that He is with us changes everything and helps us determine how to use our time on our phones. When we know He is with us, we want to act in ways that bring Him glory and show Him love, and we want others to know His presence by being around us.

As you continue in this challenge to redeem the time you spend on your phone by using your device to glorify God, remember that you are not alone. He is present with you. You have access to a good and loving Father. And because He is with you, you can always turn to Him as you wrestle with spending too much time on your phone. As you put away your phone more and more, ask Him to help you notice Him more. May His presence be all-consuming and more enthralling than your screen, and may you be known for being more attentive to Him than a device!

"
Remembering that He is with us changes everything and helps us determine how to use our time on our phones.

DO YOU OFTEN THINK ABOUT THE LORD'S PRESENCE?
WHY OR WHY NOT?

HOW WOULD THINKING ABOUT THE LORD BEING WITH YOU
CHANGE HOW YOU APPROACHED YOUR DAY-TO-DAY LIFE?

HOW WOULD THINKING ABOUT THE LORD BEING WITH YOU
CHANGE HOW YOU SPENT TIME ON YOUR PHONE?

Ways Your PHONE is Helpful

IF WE LEARN TO USE THESE DEVICES WELL, THEY CAN AID US IN LOVING THE LORD EVEN MORE.

Apps to Help You Love Your Bible

It is unlikely that we will ever return to a world in which smartphones do not exist. They are a part of our lives, and they have changed the world around us. We have to learn to use them for the glory of God. While we can misuse these devices because we are sinful, there is nothing inherently wrong with our phones. God sovereignly allowed them to be created, and He gave the creators of our phones the ingenuity and innovation to make them. They are truly astounding pieces of technology! When the first men went to the moon in the 1960s, the computer that their spaceship held had less capability than our phones do today! Everywhere we go, we can carry around powerful computers with us in our pockets and purses. If we learn to use these devices well, they can aid us in loving the Lord even more.

So what phone apps can help us love God? There are quite a few. The list you see in today's reading is not exhaustive, but it will help you begin acquiring valuable resources on your device! The apps discussed today are specifically for helping you love your Bible more.

THE DAILY GRACE CO. APP

The Daily Grace Co. offers a beautiful app for women who want to dig deeper into Scripture while experiencing community. The app will allow you to stay up to date on our podcast episodes and blog posts. Our app also holds all of our content for the online companions of our Bible studies! Here, you can also interact with other women who are completing the same studies you are.

DWELL: AUDIO BIBLE

Dwell is an audio Bible app that offers listeners multiple translations and various narrators. The app also features playlists of verses arranged by different topics and themes. Dwell lets its listeners play Scripture with the music of their choice in the background, but it is not distracting and is designed to enhance the listening experience. Please note, this app requires a subscription for a year of use.

THE BIBLE MEMORY APP

The Bible Memory App helps users memorize and meditate on Scripture and tracks your progress on verses you are trying to memorize. It also employs kinesthetic, visual, and auditory techniques to help users remember their verses.

BLUE LETTER BIBLE

The Blue Letter Bible app is probably one of the most comprehensive Bible study tools available to us on our phones! You can look up any passage or verse and dive into the Hebrew and Greek words being used. You can also read the definitions of the words, their grammatical elements, how they compare in multiple translations, and so much more! It is an amazing resource for someone who wants to dig more deeply into God's Word.

Day Twenty-One Questions

WHAT ARE SOME OF YOUR FIRST THOUGHTS WHEN YOU THINK ABOUT HOW YOU COULD GLORIFY GOD WITH YOUR PHONE?

WHAT ARE SOME OTHER APPS THAT HELP YOU LOVE THE LORD MORE? WHO COULD YOU SHARE YOUR APP LIST WITH TO ENCOURAGE THEM?

WHAT ARE SOME APPS YOU MAY NEED TO DELETE BECAUSE THEY DO NOT STIR YOUR AFFECTION FOR THE LORD?

OUR PRIMARY
SOURCE OF
SPIRITUAL GROWTH
SHOULD ALWAYS BE
FROM TIME SPENT IN
THE WORD OF GOD.

Apps for Devotional Content

Our primary source of spiritual growth should always be our time spent in the Word of God. It is easy for us to spend most of our time in secondary sources (Christian articles, blogs, podcasts, etc.) or listening to people tell us about the Bible instead of being in the Bible ourselves. The Bible is the very Word of God, and as we read it, we fellowship with God and are transformed to be more like Him. Knowing Him is the most important endeavor of our lives. While we want to ensure that most of our time is devoted to Scripture, time spent in devotional content is not at all wasted. There is much to learn from other believers who love the Lord and faithfully walk with Him. This book that you are reading now is devotional content, and these kinds of resources can no doubt be instrumental in our spiritual growth and development!

A plethora of apps exist that are incredibly beneficial. Having a folder of these apps on your home screen could be a great use of your screen time when you have some time to spare while sitting in the waiting room for a doctor's appointment or sitting in the pick-up line at your child's school.

Many of these apps offer daily devotionals and bible reading, while others offer gospel-centered content on different topics. Still others provide commentary or catechism questions and answers or allow you to read books directly from youo pohone! Many audio-books are available through some apps as well.

KNOWING HIM
IS THE MOST
IMPORTANT
ENDEAVOR OF
OUR LIVES.

DOES YOUR TIME IN THE WORD EXCEED YOUR TIME IN DEVOTIONAL CONTENT? WHY OR WHY NOT?

WHAT DEVOTIONAL CONTENT HAS BEEN THE MOST MEANINGFUL FOR YOU?

WHAT ARE SOME TOPICS RELATED TO SPIRITUAL GROWTH THAT YOU WOULD LIKE TO LEARN MORE ABOUT? WHICH APPS COULD BEST HELP YOU LEARN IN SPARE MOMENTS THROUGHOUT YOUR DAY?

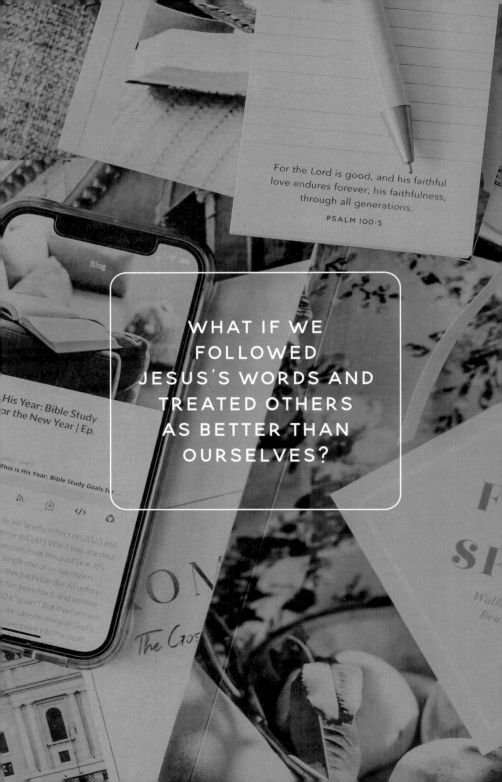

For the Lord is good, and his faithful love endures forever; his faithfulness, through all generations.

PSALM 100:5

WHAT IF WE FOLLOWED JESUS'S WORDS AND TREATED OTHERS AS BETTER THAN OURSELVES?

Apps to Help
You Love Others

While our phones easily and often become all about us, so many apps and programs are available that can help us love others well! When we really think about it, every time we interact with others through our devices is an opportunity to show the love of Jesus. We can draw them to the cross with love and graciousness, even over a screen. Online interactions between people can sometimes be anything but kind. The screen and distance between us and another cause us to sometimes temporarily forget to practice self-control. Words fly in online arguments, and social media posts become battlegrounds. In this way, the internet has become a dangerous place. But what if every time we became frustrated with someone across the screen, we thought of a way to serve them instead of lash out at them? What if every time we saw something we disagreed with online, we would pray for the person who said it and think of ways we could be gracious to them? What if we followed Jesus's words and treated others as better than ourselves?

We would fill the world with Christ's love, and we would become so familiar with the needs of others that our phones would no longer consume us as they did. Instead, we would put our phones in their proper place. When we follow in the footsteps of Jesus, everything comes under His control, even our phones.

ECHO PRAYER

Echo is a free app that allows its users to record prayers and join groups that want to share prayer requests. The app will also set reminders on your phone to remind you to pray throughout the day. This can help small groups at church interact with each other through prayer. When you receive a reminder to pray for someone, you can text to see how that person is doing and if there are any updates for the prayer request. It is certainly easy to say that you will pray for someone, but we often forget if we do not write it down.

INK CARDS

Ink Cards is a fun, easy way to send beautiful cards to people you love. This app has lots of designs, and most of the cards are inexpensive. You can save addresses to make it easier to send cards to your family and friends regularly. The cards make great keepsakes as well.

FAMILYALBUM

FamilyAlbum is a safe and secure way to share photos online with loved ones. If you do not want to share lots of photos on social media but still want to keep family up to date on moments throughout your day (especially if you have little ones), Family-Album is a great tool to use!

VENMO

Every once in a while, everyone has the urge to go pick up a fun treat! It is even better when someone stops by with a coffee or smoothie as a random surprise, but sometimes you do not live close to someone you want to surprise. Venmo is a money payment app that is run by Paypal, and it allows users to send payments to each other through their mobile devices. You can use the app to send a small amount of money to a friend as a surprise, for a birthday or special occasion, or even as a pick-me-up on a hard day! It is a simple way to show friends and family that you are thinking of them!

Day Twenty-Three Questions

WHAT IS ONE WAY YOU CAN SURPRISE SOMEONE WITH AN ACT OF KINDNESS THIS WEEK?

WHICH ONE OF THESE APPS DO YOU THINK YOU AND YOUR FAMILY MIGHT ENJOY? WHAT IS YOUR FIRST IDEA FOR HOW TO USE IT?

HOW CAN YOU SHOW CHRIST'S LOVE TO OTHERS AS YOU INTERACT WITH OTHERS ON YOUR PHONE?

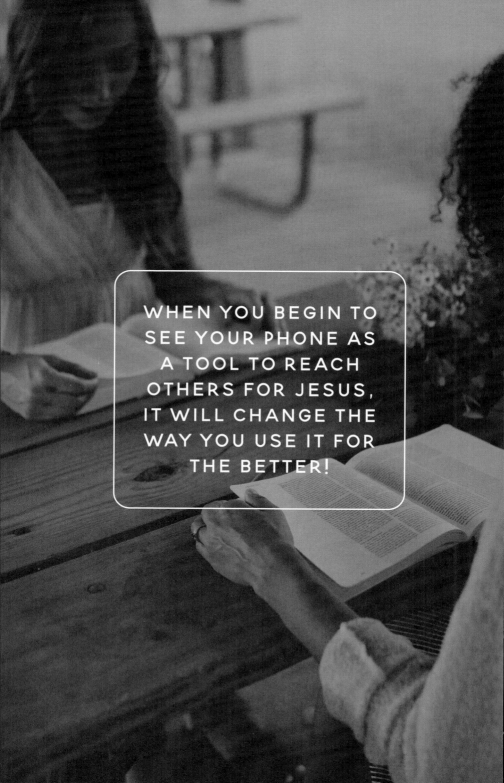

WHEN YOU BEGIN TO
SEE YOUR PHONE AS
A TOOL TO REACH
OTHERS FOR JESUS,
IT WILL CHANGE THE
WAY YOU USE IT FOR
THE BETTER!

Connecting with Family and Friends

Before the internet, smartphones, and video calls, most people who lived far away from each other could only connect by writing letters or calling someone on a landline phone. But today, we have so many ways to stay in touch with our loved ones. While the amount of possible communication can be distracting and sometimes overwhelming, the advances in technology have given us incredible blessings. We can easily maintain relationships with people who live hours from us or are across the world. We do not have to wait for a letter to come in the mail or hope that we hear someone's call to our family phone (for everyone who has only lived in a world with mobile phones, this was a corded phone that was usually found on the wall in the kitchen or common area). Getting in touch with someone is simple and attainable. What a gift from God!

So what are some ways that you can use your phone to meaningfully keep in touch with family and friends? How can you use your phone as a ministry tool to love these important people or reach out to someone you are getting to know? There are a number of ideas.

Apps like Voxer and Marco Polo allow you to send audio messages and video messages to family and friends. You could start a family group chat on Marco Polo and send videos of fun things that happen throughout the day. This could also be a great way to keep up with old friends. It does not require a scheduled video call or texts back and forth. Each person can respond when it is convenient.

Phone calls are becoming a long-lost art. Most people text back and forth, but many people still appreciate hearing a loved one's voice on the phone, especially grandparents and elderly members in your neighborhood or church. Try and call one person a week to check on them and see how they are doing. Consider someone who may not receive many phone calls, and have a couple of questions ready to ask them.

Have a list of people written out in a journal that you text once a month for prayer updates. Pick a day of the month to text them and set a monthly reminder to see if there are any updates or new prayer requests to share with you.

Go through your phone once a week, and check unread messages. Make sure you have responded to messages you may have missed during the week. There can be so much pressure to respond to texts immediately, but this does not always happen, and that is okay! Pick a time when you know you can respond to messages, and give yourself fifteen minutes to check them.

Stewarding our phones well means that we get to use them in productive, wonderful ways that edify others and encourage the body of Christ! When you begin to see your phone as a tool to reach others for Jesus, it will change the way you use it for the better!

Stewarding our phones well means that we get to use them in productive, wonderful ways that edify others and encourage the body of Christ!

WHAT IDEAS DO YOU HAVE ABOUT ENCOURAGING OTHERS WITH YOUR PHONE? ARE YOU CONSIDERING ONE OF THE IDEAS LISTED ABOVE OR A VARIATION OF IT?

WHO ARE PEOPLE YOU FEEL LED TO CONTACT? WHAT WILL YOU DO TO MAKE THEM FEEL VALUED?

HOW IS SEEING YOUR PHONE AS A MINISTRY TOOL A HELPFUL PERSPECTIVE SHIFT?

PODCASTS CAN BE
A GREAT HELP TO
OUR RELATIONSHIP
WITH THE LORD.

Podcasts

Before the year 2000, podcasts were a form of media that did not exist. The word "podcast" was created in 2004. Many of you who are reading this are probably older than the word itself. Podcasts began as a form of amateur radio and have developed to become a booming industry, more than 100 million Americans listening to them every single month. There are a variety of genres and topics in the podcast world which explains their popularity as it is easy for most people to find one that interests them.

Podcasts can be a great help to our relationship with the Lord. There are so many that aim to encourage believers about Him and teach them truth about the Word of God. But they can be an encouragement to you in other ways too! Do you want to learn how to be hospitable? To cook better meals? To organize your home? To become more productive? To understand more about the history of the world? Some podcasts address these questions and interests! There is truly a podcast for any topic you can think of, and if there is not a podcast for something you are passionate about, you can create one.

It is always important before beginning to listen to a podcast to understand the worldview from which someone is speaking. It is not bad to listen to people who may not hold your same beliefs or convictions, because as you listen to them, you can learn how to engage with people who share different opinions. A caveat to that is that if you are listening to a podcast about the Christian faith, you do want to know where a person stands before applying their counsel to your life and walk with Jesus.

The Daily Grace Co. offers two podcasts that would be great places to begin if you have not already dived into this form of media! Both of these podcasts aim to help you grow in your faith!

DAILY GRACE PODCAST

This Daily Grace Co. podcast seeks to help women know that deep Bible study, sound doctrine, and rich theology are not just for the seminary student or pastor but are accessible and transformational for all believers. This podcast covers a variety of topics and will certainly encourage you as you grow closer to Jesus. We would love for you to listen!

BIAY PODCAST

The Bible in a Year with Daily Grace walks through the entire Bible from start to finish in one year. Before you listen to the podcast each day, you can read chapters of the Bible as laid out in the *Story of Redemption* studies available at *thedailygraceco.com* or in our free yearly bible reading plan available in The Daily Grace Co. app. In each day's podcast we will briefly chat about the Bible chapters to see how they fit into God's big story of redemption, how they point to Jesus, and how we should live in response.

Day Twenty-Five Questions

WHAT TOPICS DO YOU WANT TO LEARN MORE ABOUT?
HOW COULD PODCASTS HELP YOU?

WHEN COULD YOU LISTEN TO PODCASTS? HOW COULD
THIS MAKE A CERTAIN HABIT OR CHORE FOR THE DAY
MORE ENJOYABLE? (E.G., MAKING DINNER, EMPTYING
THE DISHWASHER, OR FOLDING LAUNDRY.)

WHILE PODCASTS CAN BE EXTREMELY HELPFUL AND
ENCOURAGING, THEY DO NOT REPLACE THE WORD OF GOD.
HOW DO YOU KEEP THE WORD OF GOD YOUR PRIMARY
SOURCE IN A WORLD THAT OFFERS EVERY FORM OF MEDIA?

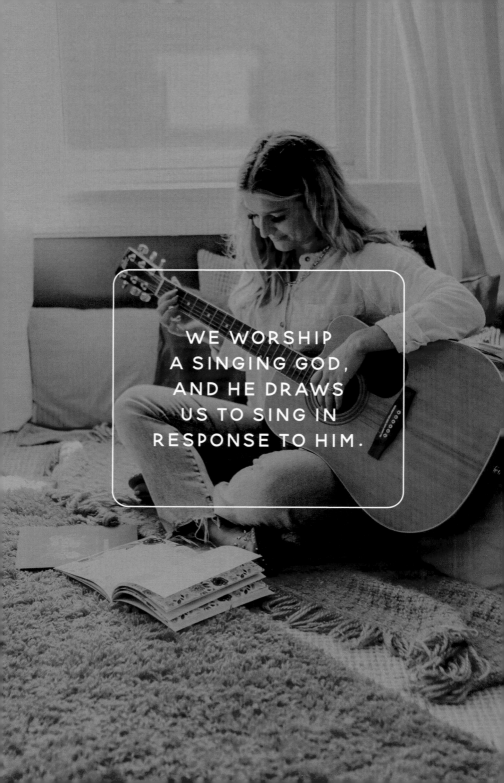

WE WORSHIP
A SINGING GOD,
AND HE DRAWS
US TO SING IN
RESPONSE TO HIM.

Music

Stereos, walkmans, CD players, mP3 players, and iPod Nanos are some of the devices we have used for the last 100 years to listen to music. Now our phones can carry all our music, and music has become even more ingrained into our culture because it goes everywhere with us. Songs contain the messages each generation wants to tell. When you listen to the most popular music of an era, you hear what people believe. In the same way, you can tell a lot about someone by the music they like.

One of the reasons people are so passionate about music is that they have been created in the image of God, and making music is something God does. In fact, Zephaniah 3:17 says the Lord sings over His creation. We worship a singing God, and He draws us to sing in response to Him. Whether people know it or not, the ability to sing and enjoy music is a gift from Him. We use these gifts to glorify and worship our Creator.

There are so many ways that you can use music on your phone to glorify God! Today we will focus just on making playlists of songs through streaming services since that is how most of us consume music.

FAMILY WORSHIP

One of the best ways to worship the Lord is with other believers, and it is even more special when those believers are your family. Singing unites the hearts of those who love the Lord and creates lasting memories for those who participate. It also allows for lots of conversation about the words in the songs that you choose. Choose two or three songs a month to sing with your family. If you have younger children, this can be a part of their bedtime routine, or these can be songs that you play as you get ready in the morning.

SONGS OF FAITHFULNESS

Music full of Scripture and truth, like classic hymns of our faith, can guide us through challenging seasons in life. What comfort is found in knowing that some of these hymns have sustained believers for hundreds of years! It is helpful to have a playlist of these hymns ready to go for difficult moments and seasons. Sometimes you need only to cry out to the Lord and be still before Him, and music can help us do that!

PLAYLIST OF THE YEAR

At the start of every year, begin creating a playlist to keep track of all of the songs you love from that year alone. How neat to look back on playlists from previous years and remember songs and the memories that accompany them. It can also be a special moment when you discover a song worthy of the year's playlist!

The ability to sing and enjoy music is a gift from Him. We use these gifts to glorify and worship our Creator.

Day Twenty-Six Questions

WHAT KINDS OF MUSIC DO YOU ENJOY? WHAT DOES THIS SAY
ABOUT THE MESSAGES YOU BELIEVE AND CARE ABOUT?

IS WORSHIP SOMETHING THAT IS A PART OF YOUR LIFE OUTSIDE
OF SUNDAY MORNING? WHY OR WHY NOT?

WHAT KIND OF SPECIAL PLAYLIST COULD YOU CREATE TO HELP
YOU WORSHIP THE LORD?

WE CAN CREATE
IDEAS AND
MEMENTOS OF
SPECIAL MEMORIES
FOR OUR FAMILY
MEMBERS.

Using Notes and Voice Memos

The notes and voice memos sections of our phone are sometimes full of random grocery lists and recordings, but these two sections of our phones can hold incredibly meaningful content for us as we go from day to day.

We create scrapbooks of our lives on our phones, whether we know it or not. If we are purposeful with how we use them, we can create ideas and mementos of special memories for our family members. This is not an aspect of our devices that is discussed often, but when you realize the potential, it can shift how you view even the most simple post on social media. The following suggestions are some ideas for you to consider!

IDEAS TO REMEMBER

When you are out and about, you may sometimes need to jot something down to remember something later. This can be anything from needing to add something to your grocery list to thinking of a plot for a good story. Having a "notepad" on your phone specifically for keeping track of random things like this is helpful. If you are on a long drive and get to a stopping point, you can turn on voice memos and just speak aloud so that you can play back your messages and remember any thoughts from earlier.

GRATITUDE LIST

Each one of us has hard days when we feel discouraged and overwhelmed. Sometimes these feelings can ruin the day if we let them, but one of the most practical action steps to take is to write out everything for which you are grateful. If you make an ongoing list as a note on your phone, you will be able to see all kinds of things you are grateful for as time passes! Imagine how large the list could be after a year of adding to it!

HOSPITALITY/BLESSINGS LIST

Consider various ways you can bless or serve other families in your church or community. If you have lots of great ideas but do not write them down, you may tend to forget them later. Have a note on your phone for these ideas so that you can actively reach people around you!

RECORDED JOURNAL

While the art of journaling can be therapeutic and a wonderful way to remember past thoughts and memories, it is not for everyone. Writing down a long page of thoughts can be quite intimidating for some, but reflection is a healthy habit to develop as a believer! Consider going to voice memos and creating a recorded journal.

IMPORTANT EVENTS

For an important event, consider setting up your phone to record a voice memo as that event plays out. It can be fun listening back to our family members discover the news or celebrate. You could record various things: family members answering special questions for each birthday, family worship sessions, or even a fun dinnertime conversation you want to hear again.

HOW DOES KNOWING THAT YOU ARE CREATING A DIGITAL SCRAPBOOK ON YOUR PHONE FOR YOUR FAMILY TO LOOK BACK ON CHANGE YOUR PERSPECTIVE ON HOW YOU USE IT?

HOW HAVE YOU USED THE VOICE MEMOS AND NOTES SECTIONS OF YOUR PHONE IN THE PAST?

WAS THERE AN IDEA ABOUT HOW TO USE VOICE MEMOS AND NOTES THAT YOU WOULD LIKE TO START IMPLEMENTING AS PART OF YOUR PLAN FOR REDEEMING YOUR PHONE TIME? HOW WILL YOU DO SO?

SAVING MEMORIES
IS PROBABLY ONE
OF THE MOST
IMPORTANT SKILLS
WE COULD LEARN
WITH OUR PHONES.

Saving Memories

By far, the quickest way we probably use up our phone's storage space is by taking way too many photos and videos and never doing a proper clean-up where we delete the ones we do not need. And since we live in a technological world, some great solutions can help you save and use these photos and videos for meaningful purposes. This is probably one of the most important skills we could learn with our phones, and it is also one of their most incredible functions. We all know that every time a new smartphone model is released, the camera is usually one of the features that companies always try to improve. It is one of their greatest marketing points, and it is one of the main reasons people switch phones. We should learn to use this feature well! Generations of family members after us will be so thankful, and you will love looking back on your memories.

PHOTO BOOKS

Photo books are simple to make as there are many online programs where you can design them from your phone or computer. To make the process less stressful for you, it may be wise to create folders on your phone of photos you would like to put in each photobook. This could be something you do in the car on a lengthy drive or even between tasks. Some people like to create a photo book every year for their family, or they create a photo book each quarter to capture more images. Whatever suits you will work! Just starting somewhere is the main point. Creating and collecting these for yourself and your family can be something everyone loves and enjoys for years to come.

YEARLY USB DRIVES

Collect videos for each of your kids from every month, and put them in a folder on your phone. At the end of the month, take the folder of videos and make it into one long video. Then transfer this video to a couple of USB drives for each child. At the end of the year, they will have a USB with twelve long videos from each month of the year. When they graduate from high school, they will have eighteen of these USB drives to take with them and treasure forever. You can repeat the same process for photos.

PHONE FLASH DRIVES

If you are ever stuck for storage space and want to move some of your photos from your phone to your computer, a great tool to use is a phone flash drive. You can easily plug them into your phone, transfer the photos, and then upload them to your computer. Or you can keep your pictures on the flash drive until you decide what you would like to do with them!

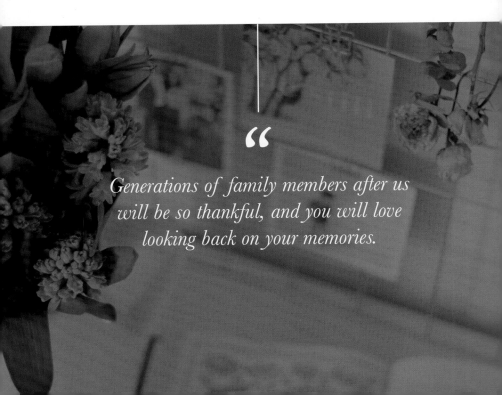

Generations of family members after us will be so thankful, and you will love looking back on your memories.

WHAT SORTS OF IDEAS DO YOU HAVE ABOUT USING AND
SAVING YOUR PHOTOS AND VIDEOS?

WHEN COULD YOU DEDICATE SOME TIME TO THIS PROJECT?
(IT IS OKAY IF IT IS NOT RIGHT AWAY - JUST THINKING ABOUT
A CERTAIN TIMEFRAME WILL GET YOU ROLLING!)

HOW WOULD A PHOTO PROJECT BENEFIT YOUR FAMILY?

Wrapping
UP

EARTH IS NOT OUR
HOME, FOR OUR
TRUE HOME IS
WITH CHRIST.

Your Phone in Light of Eternity

We have made it to the last section of this challenge and booklet! What a journey! The lessons you have learned and the habits you have practiced are so valuable to your life in this digital age. It may feel tempting to throw this booklet aside and return to your old phone habits, but be encouraged to press on. On the days when you feel like escaping from the world and scrolling on your phone, remember to view your phone in light of eternity. Your phone can be a tool in bringing you closer to the Lord, or it can severely distract you from Him and your eternal home. This is a mindset shift that changes everything for the believer. Earth is not our home, for our true home is with Christ.

When you reach eternity, your phone will no longer matter to you. Even if technology is somehow present in Jesus's kingdom, it will not be something we struggle to use with proper self-control because we will be consumed with Christ and living in His presence. Sin will no longer pervert God's creation. He has given us the ability to steward these devices well, and they can lead us to long for Christ's return. When they point our minds in this direction, we are using technology for the glory of God. We are putting away treasures in heaven and viewing our phones rightly—as tools used to honor God.

You can carry this perspective into every aspect of your life. Everything you do and say is affected when an eternal perspective governs you. Do not be fooled by your phone thinking that this life is all that matters. It is passing away quickly, and the thrills of technology are nothing compared to the beauty and splendor we will one day witness in Christ's kingdom. Learn to put your phone in its proper place, disallowing it to govern your time. When you do, you will make room in your life to truly enjoy God and the blessings He has given you. Eternity is coming! What a day that will be!

Everything you do and say is affected when an eternal perspective governs you.

Day Twenty-Nine Questions

HOW DOES HAVING AN ETERNAL PERSPECTIVE CHANGE YOUR DAY-TO-DAY LIFE?

HOW DOES HAVING AN ETERNAL PERSPECTIVE HELP YOU THINK DIFFERENTLY ABOUT YOUR PHONE?

WHEN ARE YOU MOST TEMPTED TO LOSE AN ETERNAL PERSPECTIVE? HOW CAN YOU BE CAUTIOUS OF THIS?

HE TRULY CARES
ABOUT OUR TIME
AND OUR DESIRE
TO GROW.

Reflection

Congratulations! You have made it to the end of this challenge! You have spent thirty days living intentionally with your phone. The discipline and commitment to growth you have exhibited testify to the grace of God in your life. He truly cares about our time and our desire to grow. Before you take what you have learned and further develop healthy phone habits, take time to reflect on all that you have learned so that these lessons can become life-long habits. Take your time answering these questions, and praise God for what He has done in your heart through this process!

WHAT WERE YOUR MOST CONCERNING PHONE HABITS BEFORE THIS CHALLENGE? HOW HAVE THEY CHANGED?

WHAT PHONE HABITS DO YOU WANT TO CONTINUE
TO DEVELOP?

WHAT WAS THE GREATEST WAY YOUR PHONE LED YOU TO LOVE
THE LORD MORE DURING THIS CHALLENGE?

IN WHAT WAY DID IT LEAD YOU AWAY FROM THE LORD?

DID YOU EXPERIENCE ANY CHANGES IN YOUR SCREEN TIME?

WERE THERE ANY CHANGES IN YOUR TOP APPS YOU USE FROM DAY TO DAY?

WHAT ARE NEW HABITS YOU WANT TO PRACTICE AFTER USING THIS BOOKLET?

HOW DOES LIVING WITH AN ETERNAL PERSPECTIVE HELP YOU THINK
ABOUT YOUR PHONE?

WHEN YOU ARE EIGHTY YEARS OLD, HOW WOULD YOU LIKE PEOPLE
TO REMEMBER YOU? HOW WILL YOUR PHONE FIT INTO THIS?

WHAT IS ANOTHER WAY YOU WANT TO GROW IN YOUR LOVE FOR THE
LORD USING THE RESOURCES ON YOUR PHONE?

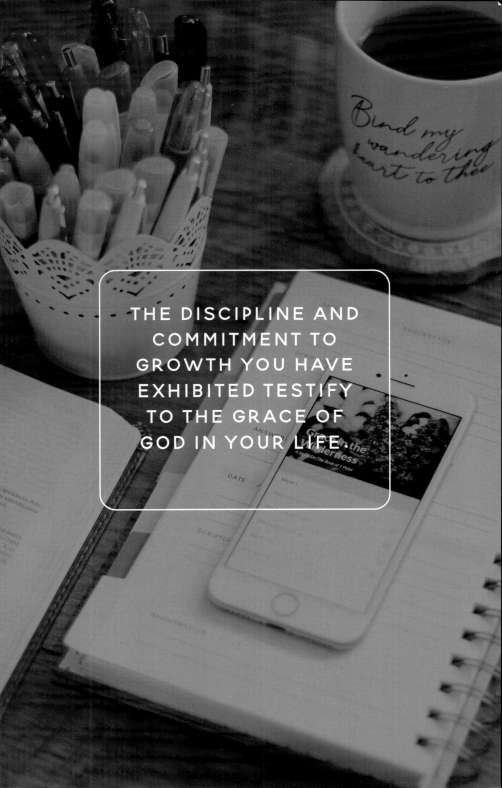

THE DISCIPLINE AND
COMMITMENT TO
GROWTH YOU HAVE
EXHIBITED TESTIFY
TO THE GRACE OF
GOD IN YOUR LIFE.

*Thank you for choosing this
resource from The Daily Grace Co.*